"In a world of work-life trade-offs, Stew Friedman offers what most think impossible: a field-tested program that gives you not only what you want in business, but also what you want in life. Brilliant!"

—Timothy Ferriss, author, *The 4-Hour Workweek*, #1 *New York Times* bestseller

"The best leaders are those who stay connected—to their communities, to the people they love, to themselves. In Stew Friedman's *Total Leadership*, you'll learn simple, powerful new ways to make these connections happen and enjoy the rich rewards that inevitably follow."

—Keith Ferrazzi, CEO, Ferrazzi Greenlight, and coauthor, *Never Eat Alone*

"In the future, being a leader will require new ways to integrate work with the rest of one's life, resulting in more effective leadership and a more fulfilling life. *Total Leadership* points the way."

—Robert Reich, professor, University of California, Berkeley; former U.S. Secretary of Labor; and author, *Supercapitalism*

"Destined to be a classic, this is a remarkable book. I have studied leadership and led organizations for over twenty years. No other book has reshaped my thinking about leadership development as much as *Total Leadership*."

—David A. Thomas, professor, Harvard Business School, and author, *Breaking Through: The Making of Minority Professionals in Corporate America*

"Stew Friedman absolutely gets it. He is both a visionary and a much-needed advocate for a new kind of leadership in the twenty-first century. What an empowering book!"

—Janet Hanson, Founder, 85 Broads

"*Total Leadership* will help you build a life, not just a résumé. Stew Friedman has written the owner's manual for all types of leaders, young and old, who aspire to both professional success and personal fulfillment."

> —Tom Tierney, Chairman and Cofounder, The Bridgespan Group, and former CEO, Bain & Company

"With a refreshingly simple approach to winning the daily struggle between family bliss and career satisfaction, Stew Friedman outlines clear and innovative solutions for better managing the competing demands of our lives. Engaging and inspiring."

> —Anne Erni, former Managing Director and Chief Diversity Officer, Lehman Brothers

"Stew Friedman brings a new definition of leadership to every sector, with 'four-way wins' that will inspire leaders at every level. A rare and moving guidebook for your journey to leadership."

> —Frances Hesselbein, Founding President and Chairman, Leader to Leader Institute, and former CEO, Girl Scouts of the USA

"As the pace of business continues to race forward at lightning speed, Stew Friedman offers us an innovative and sustainable model for successful leadership. *Total Leadership* provides a unique proposition for individuals who strive to be their very best both personally and professionally."

> —Dave Lissy, CEO, Bright Horizons Family Solutions

"It is difficult to translate the dynamic process of learning into the pages of a book, but Stew Friedman has done it! When we become more intentional leaders, it benefits every facet of our lives: our work, our families, our community connections, and, at the deepest level, ourselves."

> —Ellen Galinsky, President, Families and Work Institute

"*Total Leadership* is so aligned with my thinking as an HR executive and medical director of a global business. With practical tools and compelling stories, Friedman demonstrates how to achieve 'four-way wins' —a distinctive, important new concept for today's leaders."

—Dr. Robert W. Carr, Vice President and Corporate Medical Director, GlaxoSmithKline

"Stew Friedman defines leadership in an exciting new way that can lead not only to greater success at work, but also to greater success at home, in the community, and for yourself—with each mutually reinforcing the other."

—Raymond V. Gilmartin, professor, Harvard Business School, and former CEO, Merck & Co., Inc.

"*Total Leadership* is a rich and satisfying call to action. Tapping into his innovative work in executive education and work/family research, Friedman teaches us how to create productive work settings that also enable satisfying personal and family lives."

—Denise M. Rousseau, professor, Carnegie Mellon University, and author, *I-deals: Idiosyncratic Deals Employees Bargain for Themselves*

"Stew Friedman accomplishes something quite rare in *Total Leadership*. Through a combination of gripping narratives and lucid descriptions of his framework, he points the way to enduring satisfaction for executives and others by uniquely connecting the richest aspects of their lives."

—Mitch Wienick, Partner, Kelleher Associates, Inc., and former President/CEO, CDI Corporation

"Across nations and industries, leaders strive to juggle the multiple aspects of their lives and meet the demands of an ever-growing list of stakeholders. Friedman calls an end to this zero-sum game. Time and time again, I have seen his method generate a great return for individuals and their organizations."

—Shlomo Ben-Hur, Vice President of Leadership Development & Learning, BP International Limited

*Praise from Friedman's former students:*

"By weaving stories of real people into this engaging narrative, Stew Friedman shows you how to succeed in all areas of your life—at once. From personal experience, I know that the program in *Total Leadership* delivers profound results for both individuals and organizations."

—Harry B. Weiner, Managing Partner, On-Ramps Services

"Stew's class at Wharton transformed my development as a leader and Internet entrepreneur. This book and the exercises in it are equally powerful—I'm buying a copy for everyone in my company."

—Brett A. Hurt, Founder and CEO, Bazaarvoice

"Stew Friedman's framework is the most comprehensive and meaningful distillation of how to lead yourself and others that I have encountered. I use the precepts of *Total Leadership* in my daily life, and I'm better off for it."

—Richard Smith, Chief of Staff to the CFO, Sears Holdings Corporation, and former Army company commander and combat veteran

"Stew's class and book helped me tremendously to rediscover and re-affirm my core work values. For a journey to authenticity, this is the must-read road map for leaders and leaders to be."

—Jane Lin-Baden, CEO, Audacee Digital Inc., China

# TOTAL
## LEADERSHIP

# TOTAL

# LEADERSHIP

## Be a Better Leader, Have a Richer Life

STEWART D. FRIEDMAN

HARVARD BUSINESS REVIEW PRESS

*Boston, Massachusetts*

Copyright 2014 Stewart D. Friedman

All rights reserved

Printed in the United States of America

10 9 8 7 6 5 4 3 2 1

No part of this publication may be reproduced, stored in or introduced into a retrieval system, or transmitted, in any form, or by any means (electronic, mechanical, photocopying, recording, or otherwise), without the prior permission of the publisher. Requests for permission should be directed to permissions@hbsp.harvard.edu, or mailed to Permissions, Harvard Business School Publishing, 60 Harvard Way, Boston, Massachusetts 02163.

The web addresses referenced in this book were live and correct at the time of the book's publication but may be subject to change.

Library of Congress Cataloging-in-Publication Data

Friedman, Stewart D.

    Total leadership : be a better leader, have a richer life (with new preface) / Stewart D. Friedman

      pages cm

    ISBN-13: 978-1-62527-438-0 (paperback)

    1. Leadership—Psychological aspects. 2. Executives—Conduct of life. 3. Quality of work life. 4. Work and family. 5. Self-actualization (Psychology)—Problems, exercises, etc. I. Title.

    HD57.7.F7515 2014

    658.4'092—dc23

                                    2014014451

*For Hallie*

# CONTENTS

TABLE OF EXERCISES   ix

PREFACE TO THE PAPERBACK EDITION: THE REVOLUTION IS HERE   xi

PREFACE: HOW TOTAL LEADERSHIP CAME TO LIFE   xv


ONE   Introduction   1
*The Total Leadership Experience*


PART I   BE REAL
Act with Authenticity


TWO   Clarify What's Important to You   29

THREE   Take the Four-Way View   53


PART II   BE WHOLE
Act with Integrity


FOUR   Respect the Whole Person   73

FIVE   Talk to Your Stakeholders   97

## PART III BE INNOVATIVE
### Act with Creativity

SIX Design Experiments 121

SEVEN Bring Others Along with You 149

---

EIGHT Conclusion 171
*Reflect and Grow*

## APPENDIXES

A Your Total Leadership Coaching Network 201

B Scoring Four-Way Wins with Total Leadership in Your Organization 211

C Further Reading 217

NOTES 227

ACKNOWLEDGMENTS 229

CHARACTER INDEX 235

GENERAL INDEX 237

ABOUT THE AUTHOR 247

# TABLE OF EXERCISES

Your Goals for the Total Leadership Program   24


PART I   BE REAL: ACT WITH AUTHENTICITY

Where Have You Come From?   32
Your Leadership Vision   41
Your Core Values   46
Pause and Reflect on What's Important   51
The Four-Way Attention Chart   57
The Four Circles   61
Domain Satisfaction—
       Your Four-Way Happiness Rating   67
Pause and Reflect on Your Four-Way View   70


PART II   BE WHOLE: ACT WITH INTEGRITY

Who Matters Most?   76
Expectations Stakeholders Have of You   78
Expectations You Have of Stakeholders   81
See Your Life as a System You Can Change   86
Forms of Communication   93

Refine Your Approach   102

Uncover Underlying Interests and
  New Ways of Meeting Expectations   108

Get Inside Their Heads and Hearts   110

Talk, Take Notes, and Reflect   117

## PART III   BE INNOVATIVE: ACT WITH CREATIVITY

Identify Possible Four-Way Wins   131

Choose the Most Promising   133

Set Your Game Plans   135

Create Scorecard—Goals   139

Create Scorecard Metrics   146

Get in the Game! Act, Adjust, Act, Adjust . . .   152

Serve *Their* Interests   161

Identify the Missing Pieces in Your Network   165

Grow Your Network   168

Review Your Scorecards   174

Review Stakeholder Expectations   178

Review What's Important   180

Return to Your Baseline   184

Distill Your Leadership Lessons   185

Your Development as Student and Coach   194

Tell Your Story   197

# The Revolution Is Here

I T HAS BEEN almost six years since the publication of *Total Leadership*, and so much has changed in our world. Indeed, we are in the midst of revolutionary changes in the leadership landscape: social, cultural, political, technological, and economic shifts that make the concepts and methods described in this book even more relevant today.

Since June 2008 we've experienced the Great Recession, rapid acceleration of the dominance of digital connectivity, undeniable changes in our global climate, the election of the first African American U.S. president, powerful new voices in the conversation about gender and the workplace, Millennials rising to bring an urgent sense of social responsibility to their careers (it's now harder to get a job at Teach for America than at Goldman Sachs), and a near-universal feeling of being constantly overwhelmed—to name just a few. People, young and old, are hungrier now than when this book first appeared for useful knowledge to help them achieve higher levels of performance and fulfillment, not just at work, but in all aspects of their lives. And that hunger is a good thing, in my estimation, for we're all capable of growing our leadership capacity and having a richer life, throughout our short time on this beautiful earth.

So it's perhaps not surprising that, after its national best-seller launch, *Total Leadership* continues to draw a wide audience, not just in the United States but worldwide and in many other languages. My new MOOC (massive open online course), available on coursera.org and based on this book, has over fifty thousand students enrolled worldwide. I've brought the concepts and tools described in *Total Leadership* to many different kinds of organizations—UnitedHealth Group, Target, the U.S. Army, the U.S. Departments of State and Labor, General Electric, eBay, Deloitte, Google, Citibank, and GlaxoSmithKline, among others—in Europe, South America, Asia, and the Middle East and built a privacy-protected social learning site where thousands of people can work in small groups to coach each other as they progress through the exercises.

Most heartening has been the response by students, not just at the Wharton School, where I've had the privilege of teaching since 1984, but at the many colleges and universities around the world where the book is now part of the curriculum. So many more women *and* men are now eager to invest their attention and effort in the process of diagnosing what matters most to them, engaging in meaningful dialogue with the people who matter most in their lives, and then discovering through creative experimentation new ways to live that are consistent with their core values and personal aspirations. They want to be part of a community of like-minded people who are finding ways to achieve what they truly want while also making the world better in some way.

I have worked with and heard from thousands of people who, with the help of this book, have gained greater competence and confidence in creating change that is truly sustainable in their lives. As an organizational psychologist, I have been very gratified to see how this systematic series of exercises can transform the way people think about what's possible. My hope is that with this paperback edition, more people will find practical ideas for action that they can use to pursue four-way wins—to improve their performance at work, at home, in the community, and for the private self (mind, body, and spirit) by finding mutual value among these disparate pieces of their lives. The world needs you to lead.

Stew Friedman
May 19, 2014

# How Total Leadership
# Came to Life

B Y THE MID-1980s, my professional life was humming. I had finished my graduate work in organizational psychology, begun research on leadership development, and landed my dream job at the Wharton School. But my wife, Hallie, and I had been trying unsuccessfully to have a child for some time.

Then, finally, at 5:30 a.m. on a beautiful autumn morning, our first child, Gabriel, arrived. In a warmly lit room in Pennsylvania Hospital I stood transfixed, holding this practically perfect being for the first time. Wrapped in a yellow blanket that covered him entirely except for his calm face, Gabriel looked at me and around the room, taking it all in. I wondered, What must I now do to make our world a safe and nurturing one for him?

I could not get this thought out of my head. A week later, I arrived back in my Wharton MBA class on organizational behavior and set aside the topic for which we'd all prepared that day, on motivation and reward systems. Instead, I told the story of what had just happened to me. I tried to extract the meaning my story might have for these talented students and incipient business leaders. "What responsibility do you have," I asked, "for creating work environments that help to cultivate the next generation? What will you do, as a business professional, to weave the strands of work, family, community, and self into the fabric of your own life?"

I don't remember much of the details of that class session—it's a blur—but I do remember the vehement reactions it evoked. About half the class scoffed, unwilling to see personal life as a relevant topic in a business school. The other half thanked me for raising such questions and for bringing more of myself to our collective dialogue.

I didn't know it then, but that moment changed my career. By giving voice to my feelings about what was important in my own life, and connecting them to the interests of others, I began a new journey. I saw how my professional role was *enhanced* by who I was in other aspects of my life, and I refocused my research to reflect the importance of bringing the whole person to work. I saw more clearly that, for me, understanding the interplay between work and the rest of life wasn't just personal, it was my calling.

Some years later, in the early 1990s, I spoke on the topic of careers at a meeting of the Academy of Management, a scholarly organization for faculty in business schools. I talked about how fatherhood had changed my career. I spoke about decisions such as giving up opportunities for tenure-track positions in favor of staying in Philadelphia for the sake of my family. Again, I found that in telling my life story I was enriching my work, this time by giving voice to similar themes in the lives of my colleagues. I made some friends that day, people who appreciated hearing about an alternative to the standard academic career model. I was learning lessons first-hand about the value of authenticity, integrity, and creativity.

At this time, I was immersed in the chaotic world of large-scale organization change. As the first director of the Wharton Leadership Program,

I was trying to create a new model of business education for Wharton, one that encouraged students to question their assumptions about career success. Students kept journals and provided feedback to each other. It was challenging—sometimes uncomfortable—for everyone involved. We at the Leadership Program felt our initiative was significant not just because it was new, but because it took an approach to leadership that responded to a real need and that attempted to integrate "telling your story" into the learning process.

We explored the intersection of career and life interests, using data we were generating through the Wharton Work/Life Integration Project, an initiative that gathered information from thousands of students and alumni. We were making connections between leadership development and personal-life challenges. Sparks flew. Students had to think about ways of forging careers that fit with their deepest values. In workshops I ran for business professionals on how to integrate work and personal lives—and how to find solutions that worked for individuals as well as for their businesses—I found an unquenchable thirst for useful knowledge, especially (but not only) among women.

At the same time, I was also consulting with companies committed to leadership development. The business world was embracing the idea that learning leadership was not just possible, but imperative to fostering organizational vitality. My work included designing educational experiences for nascent leaders and blending these experiences into a company's career-advancement system.

As an outgrowth of these activities, I was invited to create a leadership academy for a major American manufacturer. In 1999, I left academia to test my ideas in a corporate setting. The new CEO wanted to connect leadership development with the need to help employees find better ways of integrating work with the rest of life. Such integration was essential to attracting and retaining the best people. Our programs were dedicated to learning leadership by doing it, and we had to ensure that each of our participants produced value for the company while at the same time growing as leaders. We wanted them to think creatively about enhancing the company's value to consumers, but we also wanted participants to see themselves in a new light—as reinvented, more confident leaders.

One program for high-potential middle managers focused on what was then called the "new economy"; it needed to prepare people to lead in the burgeoning digital world. As this program's purpose crystallized, it dawned on me that we could imagine new technology in the service of developing leadership capacity for *all* of life. *Total leadership* became my shorthand for a new way to think about leadership, from the point of view of the whole person.

Participants in all our programs were required to undertake some form of creative challenge, some new initiative. For this program, the initial goal we set was to *improve business results by enriching lives*. We would, as this apparently paradoxical purpose suggests, produce improved performance at the company by integrating work more effectively into the whole life of the developing leader. That leader would, in turn, create opportunities for others to do the same in the company, and beyond.

We created something new: a program that starts and ends with the person—not the business person, but the whole person. Since returning to Wharton in 2001, I've refined this program while offering it to business students and professionals in a variety of settings around the world. I have come to see that the point of the Total Leadership program is to create what I now call "four-way wins"—better results at work, at home, in the community, *and* for your self.

My purpose in this book is to bring the possibility of four-way wins to you, showing you step-by-step how to be a better leader by having a richer life and how to have a richer life by being a better leader.

## CHAPTER 1

# Introduction

## *The Total Leadership Experience*

TOTAL LEADERSHIP is a novel synthesis of ideas that have emerged from two traditionally separate fields: the study of leadership and the study of how individuals can find harmony among the different parts of their lives. This book presents a fresh approach for developing leadership *and* it offers a new method for integrating work, home, community, and self.

It is designed to work for anyone, at any organizational level and in any career stage, whether college student or CEO, insurance salesman or PTA president, bakeshop owner or investment banker. The Total Leadership program is for you if you sense that you are succeeding in one aspect of life while underperforming in the others, or failing to capture value from one part of life and bringing it to bear in others, or living with too much conflict among your different roles. Instead, with Total Leadership you seek "four-way wins": results that are meaningful not only for your work and career, *or* for your home and family, *or* for your community and society, *or* for your self, but for *all* these seemingly disparate domains of your life.

This book is based on many years of research as well as real-world, practical knowledge. I have coached thousands of people using the Total Leadership approach. If you're like the people I've worked with at Wharton and elsewhere, this book will help you *perform better* according to the standards of the most important people in your life, *feel better* in all the domains of your life, and have *greater harmony* among the domains because you will have more resources at your disposal to fit the parts of your life together. You'll achieve more and more four-way wins because you'll be a more inspired, effective leader.

Learning the Total Leadership method and producing four-way wins is possible for anyone willing to practice *being real* (acting with authenticity), *being whole* (acting with integrity), and *being innovative* (acting with creativity). Leadership can—indeed must—be learned. It is learned by taking action toward a direction you choose, gaining support, exercising skills, reflecting on your experience, and then coaching others. Each of these steps is outlined in this book. And you can always get better at leadership, much as a master musician is always perfecting the tools of her craft. Right from the beginning, then, and through each successive chapter, I will show you how to practice the Total Leadership method and so enhance your skills and your impact.

But first let me introduce you to a couple of the people you'll meet throughout the book, most of whom were students in my course at the Wharton School, ranging from a twentysomething Asian American marketing professional in San Francisco to an over-fifty CEO who emigrated from the Middle East to Washington, D.C., to start a technology company. These characters (all of whom are disguised) will guide you on each step along the journey you're about to begin.

## • How Total Leadership Helps

"I like my work," wrote Jenna Porter at the beginning of a workshop she took in 2005. "It gives me a sense of purpose, an opportunity to encounter and influence people in ways that make me feel good about the world I'm living in. But spending so much energy on my career has made other areas of my life fall short of my expectations."

A forty-eight-year-old mother of three children, Jenna worked at the time as a manager at a small real estate consulting firm in Philadelphia. She enjoyed considerable success. And yet, like many people who pick up this book, she wasn't satisfied with how things were going in her life. She reflected further: "Work infringes completely on the quantity and quality of the time I spend with my family. I've missed out on too much of my children's lives. And I've allowed other areas of my life to suffer. I'm too busy to read, go hear live music, or do other things I love, and I've only managed to promote my physical health—like walking in the woods—for short periods of time. I can't help thinking that my work suffers from the dissatisfaction I feel elsewhere."

Jenna had numerous responsibilities beyond work. She had many people who mattered to her and to whom she mattered, starting with her partner of twenty years and their adopted children, who were seventeen, thirteen, and nine. But her sense of overwhelming responsibilities and pinched satisfaction had been growing, and was exacerbated by the fact that Jenna's father was dying of pancreatic cancer. She wanted to change her work situation to free up time to care for him with her sister, with whom she had always been close, without sacrificing precious time with her partner and children. In the old days, the only way she knew to achieve some satisfaction in her life at work and in her life away from work was to trade off one area for another, in a chase after some kind of *balance*. But that search—with the demands of employees, kids, partner, sister, and father—seemed more and more futile.

After her four months of practicing my Total Leadership program, though, Jenna changed. She exchanged her frequent feelings of being distracted and irritable for feelings of being more fully engaged both at work and in her life beyond work. She no longer felt passive. She reduced the internal conflict that had been weighing her down, and began to focus on things that really mattered to her.

Most importantly, Jenna began to think of herself as a leader, in *all* parts of her life. How did Jenna so transform herself in such a short time? She discovered, in a frank conversation with her boss, that he cared for her and her desire to attend to her father. He was also concerned about *her* health. This emboldened her to take steps to reconfigure her work arrangements in ways she had never before considered. She came to see for the first time that because her coworkers depended on her, she could depend on them in ways she hadn't thought of before. Jenna created new freedom for herself at work by delegating to those who not only *could* take on new responsibilities but who *benefited* from doing so, for their own growth and success. She adjusted her schedule so that she could focus on the most important aspects of her job, help her sister care for their ailing father, and find time for taking a few long walks each week. In short, she became a better leader—more real, more whole, and more innovative.

Jenna works fewer hours today than she did in 2005, but she's more productive. Not only do her boss and coworkers benefit, but her family does, too. Her physical and emotional well-being has improved. For Jenna, the Total Leadership program provided a way to create small changes at work (delegating more and spending less time at the office) that produced better performance all the way around—four-way wins. She learned how to work with colleagues and connect with her family and community in new ways, enlisting support by ensuring that others benefited also from changes she was making. She's a new kind of leader.

André Washington, a thirty-three-year-old from Seattle, came to my Total Leadership course with a different set of frustrations. A product manager at a major technology firm, he was seen by higher-level executives as someone with a bright future in the company. At six feet, André projects confidence without being intimidating. He has a balding pate and close-cropped hair. His alert eyes focus intently on audiences large or small. He listens well, and when he speaks, he does so with a voice that conveys authority.

> I see myself as introspective and self-aware, and also open to change. I feel a strong pressure to achieve and succeed, especially financially. It's not an overburdening pressure; I welcome it. I feel capable—even, in some ways, destined—to achieve exceptional success, to contribute and to make an impact, particularly within my community.
>
> But something is missing. Yes, I'm successful, but I just don't feel as if I've reached my full potential. I like my job, but I sense stagnation creeping in. I'm leaving a lot on the table in terms of both my ability to contribute as well as the quality of my contribution. I'm underperforming, and that cheats me, my family, and other people I care about. I need to make some changes, not just to feel better but to do things that genuinely benefit all the areas of my life.

At the start of his Total Leadership experience, André wrote about a future that was consistent with values in which he believed strongly but by that time had gone "largely unexpressed." He set out to share with others this image of his desired future in order to test his ideas and win their support. He started with his wife, who had long wished that André had more time to spend with her and their two rambunctious girls, ages six and two. He also conveyed it to his mother and sister, who were financially and emotionally dependent on him.

Then André tried some experiments that would establish a greater "sense of true purpose." He took a first step toward realizing his "ultimate career objective"—a chain of upmarket salons predominantly serving black women—by working with his wife to research both the market potential and how to raise seed capital. He experimented with using technology to communicate more efficiently with his current work team, which helped him to be more effective in his current job and gave him valuable experience that he might apply when, in the future, he founded the new business with his wife. He began to take swimming lessons, along with his two-year-old daughter, which fulfilled a long-held wish, gave him a practical skill, boosted his confidence, and enhanced his relationship with his younger child.

André's Total Leadership journey brought marked results. "I not only perform better overall, but I feel better," he says, four months after starting out. In using his time more intelligently, he's now a more valuable asset to his current employer. He took the steps toward his new career goal with his wife. Their relationship improved, as did hers with her family and friends far away. He's doing things that make him happier; he's inspired. Perhaps paradoxically, his energy at work is greater now than it was before because he's looking forward through a new lens.

Jenna and André are very different people, of course, yet they are typical of those I meet every day in classes and workshops. What they have in common is that they are successful by some standards, but want to perform better and do more of the things that matter most to them. They want to be better leaders and have richer lives.

People like Jenna and André—and you—try the Total Leadership program for a variety of reasons. Some feel unfulfilled and unhappy because they're not doing what they love. Some don't feel genuine. Too many of their daily responsibilities and activities are inconsistent with what they value and who they really want to be. They're unfocused and so they lack a sense of purpose, infused with meaning and passion.

Some have a sense of being disconnected; they feel isolated from people who matter to them. The parts of their lives don't seem to fit together into a whole, so they're overwhelmed and pulled in too many directions. They feel stressed and unable to accomplish important tasks on time because they're distracted or overextended. They resent doing what others want, not what they want; or, on the flip side, they feel guilty for not doing enough for others. They despair that people at work don't see them as leaders who contribute to others' success. They crave stronger relationships, built on trust, and yearn for enriched social networks beyond those that now seem narrow. They want to feel more connected, to belong.

Some are in a rut. They want to find something new that taps their creative energy and engages them, but they lack the clarity—and the courage—to do so. They feel as if they're not moving forward. They lack the skills to manage the torrents of information flooding their everyday lives, making it impossible to realize the promise of new media for greater freedom. They feel out of control and lack the kind of flexibility they need to fit it all in.

Despite such frustrations, many of us feel compelled to make our world better—to lead more effectively in all aspects of our lives. The concrete steps laid out in this book show you how to do this, to tap your energy for creating meaningful change and enjoy the fruits of your own transformation.

## Total Leadership Yields Real Results

Total Leadership came to fruition when I was recruited to head up a leadership development program at a *Fortune* 50 company. We started with thirty-five high-potential managers from across the globe. They followed all the steps in the Total Leadership program and, in the span of about four months, implemented changes that touched work and the other parts of their lives. Their experiments produced a combined $5.8 million in cost savings, $0.7 million in new revenue, and $0.5 million in productivity gains.[1]

In addition to the quantifiable dollar results, these business professionals improved their relationships with customers and colleagues, and felt more satisfied with their jobs. They felt more deeply connected to their families and their communities, especially since they had drawn them into the process of change. They reported feeling healthier and less stressed. They were making better use of leisure time. And they were feeling better about the company and more excited about tying their futures to its future.

They accomplished these results not by instituting lean manufacturing or quality-control programs like Six Sigma. They did it by reframing the idea of business leadership, by applying new skills and insights at work, at home, in the community, and within the self.

By now many more people have tested my Total Leadership method in classes at the Wharton School and in workshops around the world. They find that by proceeding through a guided series of exercises and experiences, they can make changes that allow them to focus their time and energy better. Their core values surface, allowing them to transform the way they allocate their attention, skills, and resources. As a result, their daily actions become more closely aligned with their values. They work smarter, with greater focus and commitment. They achieve the results that matter to them most, in *all* areas of their lives.

I have asked hundreds of participants to compare how they assess their satisfaction before and after they've taken themselves through Total Leadership. Their levels of satisfaction increase by an average of 20 percent in their work lives, 28 percent in their home lives, and 31 percent in their community lives. Perhaps most significantly, their satisfaction with their own interior lives—physical, emotional, intellectual, and spiritual—increases by 39 percent. Similarly, they report that they believe their own performance at work, at home, in their communities, and within themselves has improved, respectively, by 9, 15, 12, and 25 percent.

Both satisfaction *and* performance get better.

Total Leadership is not an abstract idea: it is a structured method that produces measurable change. You become more focused on the things that matter, and so you feel more grounded, more like the person you want to be. You generate more support and feel more connected to the important people in your life. You become more resilient in response to the vagaries of our turbulent world. And you become more open to discovery and so feel more hopeful, indeed enthusiastic, about the future and your power to shape it.

**FIGURE 1-1**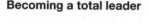

**Becoming a total leader**

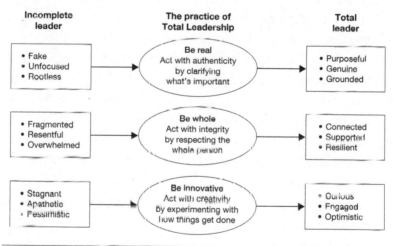

## Learning the Practice of Total Leadership in This Book

Through the exercises you'll do and the guidance I'll provide, you will improve your leadership ability and impact by practicing these principles, to which the three parts of this book correspond.

### Be Real: Act with Authenticity

Acting with authenticity gives you the strength that comes from doing what you love, drawing on the resources of your whole life, knowing that you're creating value for your self, your family, your business, your world. Effective leaders articulate a vision—a compelling image of an achievable future—that inspires them and the people around them. Their everyday actions fit not only with their personal values but also with the values of the groups of which they are a part. Through continual observation and reflection, they know their priorities, their strengths and weaknesses. They increase commitment to common goals by genuinely talking and listening to the people they care most about. And they hold themselves and others accountable for pursuing valued goals.

In part 1 you'll explore what it means for you to be real, to clarify what's important. You'll start, in chapter 2, by writing about how crucial events in your past have shaped your values and about your aspirations for your life in the future. In chapter 3, you'll take what I call the "four-way view" by assessing the relative importance of work, home, community, and self; how much you actually focus time and attention to each of these parts of your life; how satisfied you are with them; and how well the goals you pursue in them are aligned with each other. This is the foundation for authenticity and for everything that follows: knowing what really matters to you.

### Be Whole: Act with Integrity

Acting with integrity satisfies the craving for a sense of connection, for coherence in the disparate parts of life, and for the peace of mind that comes from adhering to a consistent code. Effective leaders take responsibility for recognizing and respecting the value of all aspects of life. They align the interests of different people in gaining support for common goals. They maintain the boundaries that enable value to be created at work as well as in other aspects of life. They nurture social networks and partnerships that provide the support needed for achieving meaningful results.

In part 2, then, you'll explore *who* really matters to you. First, in chapter 4, you'll identify the most important people in your life and what you expect of them as well as what they expect of you. You'll think through how these performance expectations affect each other, looking perhaps for the first time at these central relationships in your life as an interdependent system, and asking whether this system has integrity, whether and how the pieces fit together as a whole. Then, in chapter 5, you'll think about how you use different forms of communication to connect with these "key stakeholders," as I call them, and then you'll prepare for and conduct dialogues with each, to verify your assumptions and to see what things look like through their eyes. This is often the most challenging part of the Total Leadership program, and the most rewarding, as you gain new insight about what really matters to your most important people.

### Be Innovative: Act with Creativity

Acting with creativity allows you to adapt to fit new circumstances, gives you confidence to try new ways of doing things, and keeps you vital. Effective leaders continually rethink the means by which goals are achieved; they keep a results-driven focus while providing maximum flexibility (choice in how, when, and where things get done). They have the courage to experiment with new arrangements and communications tools to better meet the expectations of people who depend on them. They don't rely on face time for getting things done, but use it wisely while taking advantage of the flexibility and control afforded by new media.

With a new, clearer perspective on what and who matters most, you've set the stage for what is the usually most enjoyable part of the process: part 3, on being innovative, in which you'll design and implement smart experiments—based on all that you've learned in the process so far—to produce better results in all parts of your life. As I describe them in chapter 6, there are nine types of Total Leadership experiments. In taking well-considered action to create meaningful, lasting change, you'll discover in chapter 7 invaluable lessons about how, as a leader, to bring others along with you in the direction you've chosen by serving their interests as well as your own—by making them win while you win.

Finally, in chapter 8, you'll carefully review what you've done to distill the lessons you've learned. You'll assess the impact of your experiments on your performance and ask what worked, what didn't, and why. You'll take a fresh look at the expectations of your key stakeholders and at your values and aspirations. And you'll see for yourself what these insights mean for what you can do to continue your growth as a successful leader intent on having a rich life.

But before we embark on this journey, let me explain what I mean when I'm talking about leadership, then very briefly review the intellectual and historical roots of the Total Leadership program and why I think it's an approach that makes sense in today's business world.

## Redefining Leadership—Bringing the Whole Person In

A common definition is that *leaders mobilize people toward valued goals.*

This book focuses on valued goals in all domains of life—four-way wins—as opposed to the traditional view of understanding leadership in one domain at a time, in isolation of the others. Valued goals in any one domain are more likely to be achieved to the extent that all four domains —work, home, community, and self—are addressed as an interdependent system. You are more effective as a leader, better able to mobilize people toward a goal, if you view that goal in the context of other goals in other domains. This does not mean that you *must* address multiple domains in order to mobilize people toward valued goals; only that you will be more effective if you do.

And who are those we call leaders? There is growing recognition in leadership theory and practice that (a) the potential for expressing leadership—for doing what leaders do—is not the sole province of managers and executives but is, rather, universal and, furthermore, that (b) groups and organizations benefit—that is, their aims are more likely to be met—when all members feel like leaders, seeing themselves as capable of mobilizing people toward valued goals. Leadership is a limitless resource: the more the better.

Being a leader, therefore, is not the same as being a middle manager or a top executive. Being a leader means inspiring committed action that engages people in taking intelligent steps, in a direction you have chosen, to achieve something that has significant meaning for all relevant parties—to win, in other words. Individuals can do this whether they are at the top, middle, or bottom of an organization or group. And they can do this in businesses, families, friendship networks, communities, and social associations.

This is not to say, of course, that the range of discretion, available resources, and breadth of impact are the same for individual contributors with no one below them, as for top executives. At different levels a leader's discretion, resources, and impact vary:

- **Individual contributor:** me and my world (work, home, and community)

- **Middle manager:** me and my world, including my direct reports

- **Top executive:** me and my world, including my organization

But four-way wins can happen at any level. The term *leader* refers to any individual who chooses to try to mobilize people toward valued goals. Everyone has the potential to lead, and to do so in all aspects of life. *Leader* in its most important sense means being the agent of your own life, influencing the things you care about most in the world to make it a richer life.

Total Leadership challenges—and changes—the way you think about yourself as a leader. This book teaches a method for enhancing the capacity to be real, to be whole, and to be innovative—the essential qualities of a total leader—that is customized to the individual. So, for example, a fifty-four-year-old senior manager's experience in reading it will be very different from a twenty-two-year-old student's. Yet both will learn about what being real, being whole, and being innovative means for them; both will learn how to achieve four-way wins in their own lives.

Like other alumni of the Total Leadership program, you will see the connections between every area of your life, knowing that the best rewards come from integrating them rather than trading off between them. And you will perform *better* at work because it fits in a more meaningful way with your family life, your role in society, and your needs for health and fulfillment. As a leader, you'll find new ways to make things better. Leadership in business, after all, isn't just about business. It's about life.

## Redefining Work/Life—
## Individuals Pursuing Four-Way Wins

The Total Leadership method is about having a richer life, but it is *not* about "work/life balance." An image of two scales in balance is the wrong metaphor. First, it suggests that we need equal amounts of competing elements to create a constant equilibrium, and for many people, equality in the importance of and attention to the different parts of life makes no sense.[2] Second, it signifies trade-offs: gaining in one area at the expense of another. Even though it is sometimes unavoidable, thinking about work and the rest of life as a series of trade-offs is fundamentally counterproductive. When the goal is work/life balance, you're forced to play a zero-sum game.

The quixotic quest for balance restricts many of us. A better metaphor for our quest comes from the jazz quartet: becoming a total leader is analogous to playing richly textured music with the sounds of life's various instruments. It is *not* about muting the trumpet so the saxophone can be heard. Unless you seek ways to integrate the four domains of your life and find the potential for each part to help produce success in the others, you cannot then capitalize on synergies in places most of us don't see or hear.

It's certainly true that over the past few decades work/life advocates have produced major gains with social policies and corporate programs designed to make it easier for working men and women to lead full and productive lives.[3] Unfortunately, though, work/life programs are often viewed as pitting the interests of business against those of other parts of life. We need to drop the slash and look instead to four-way wins. If we pursue four-way wins, we clarify from the start that all constituents must gain for any one of them to gain.

Many work/life policies and programs are driven from the top down and standardized, for the sake of equality. But one size can't possibly fit all. Individuals (at all levels) must act to create meaningful change, whether or not supportive policies are in place. Individuals—in their different ways, in their different circumstances—must integrate work with the rest of life. Total Leadership represents a new step in the evolution of the work/life field: it is a systematic method for producing four-way wins that is tailored to fit the lives of individuals.

## Roots: Twentieth-Century Sources for Total Leadership

Since the dawn of human consciousness, people have been trying to understand the twin interests of this book: how to mobilize people to produce meaningful change and how to live a good and complete life. A survey of source ideas might start with the mythic Gilgamesh and take us through Moses's trials in the desert, the education of Plato's philosopher-king, the transcendentalism of Emerson and Thoreau, and Karl Marx's theses on power and the means of production.

The immediate intellectual roots of the Total Leadership approach were formed more recently, by twentieth-century scholars who explored such fundamental questions as: What is leadership and why does it matter? How does work fit with the rest of life? How do organizations cultivate productive people? How do people and organizations learn and change? Let's review each very briefly.[4]

### What Is Leadership and Why Does It Matter?

An early thrust in leadership studies focused on traits, arguing that good leaders exhibit certain qualities, like initiative, optimism, confidence, persistence, self-awareness, a willingness to make paramount the needs of others, a sense of purpose, the ability to encourage others, the ability to delegate, and an understanding of others' points of view. Researchers focused on how to match different leadership styles to fit the demands of different situations. In the 1990s, theories of emotional and social intelligence emerged as researchers sought models of leadership that encompassed the personal: leadership studies began to focus on the person within the leader and the value of connecting with the basic humanity of others.

What is it that leaders do that's so important? They inspire commitment to produce results that matter to the collective, whether through the "path-goal" model of leadership, in which a leader clears the path toward the goal of the group by meeting the needs of subordinates, or through the experimental model, in which leaders bring people together to improve a group, an organization, or society.

The "human potential movement" of the 1960s, with its emphasis on empowering the individual, challenged the notion of the leader as one man on high exhorting the troops below. Leadership is no longer just about people at the top of the pyramid. In the last four decades, moreover, new approaches have increasingly focused on values that run deeper than one's performance at work.

### How Does Work Fit with the Rest of Life?

While research on leadership was evolving, organizational psychologists and sociologists were rethinking the different roles we fill and how they affect each other. In the 1960s, scholars began to apply role theory and systems analysis to understanding organizations and the lives of the people in them.[5] Other researchers in the 1970s wrote about the connections between work and family life in society and in organizations.[6] The field of "work/family" developed, as researchers focused attention on child-rearing as an issue for business and children were reimagined as "the unseen stakeholders at work."[7]

In the last two decades this field—now called "work/life"—has expanded to include researchers not only from child development and organizational psychology but also from labor economics and law, business strategy, cultural anthropology, public policy, family systems, and international management. Researchers have developed new models for understanding how people and organizations manage the dynamic tensions among different roles in life. The focus until very recently, however, has been on models that presume conflict between work and the rest of life. Increasingly, we are learning about how we must not view any particular part of life in isolation but, rather, as part of an interdependent system of roles with potential for both mutual enrichment and depletion.

### How Do Organizations Cultivate Productive People?

Another body of ideas evolved to reverse the industrial trend toward dehumanized and dehumanizing work that resulted from the assembly line and bureaucratic organization structures. Business leaders came to realize that the economic model of the worker as a mere extension of the machine was destructive—and it reduced motivation and productivity. By the 1960s, people in all fields were discovering new means for the expression of individual initiative and talent in the service of collective ends. The fields of human resources and organization development grew, focused on improving conditions at work in order to increase both job *and* life satisfaction. Current practices such as workplace flexibility reflect theories that emerged then about how to design work so that it makes sense for the individual and the organization.

The 1990s saw a growing number of researchers study what's now called "human capital"—the value individuals bring to business enterprises; not only technical skills, but intangibles like passion and teamwork. The idea that investment in people means investing in "whole people" has gained currency. Analyses of the new worker increasingly focus on both work and other parts of life, and on fresh conceptions of what "good work" means. Authors rooted in spiritual traditions have contributed by emphasizing the importance of meaningfulness in work and organization life.

### How Do People and Organizations
### Learn and Change?

Thought on the nature of leadership and the pursuit of happiness inside and outside of work has been profoundly shaped by scientists of the mind—from Sigmund Freud to Carl Rogers—and by researchers who began to apply ideas about psychology and the capacity for personal growth to leaders in organizations. John Gardner wrote eloquently about what he learned from his experiences as an executive in business and government, emphasizing how the lifelong pursuit of self-knowledge is *the* leadership imperative, for it is the basis of self-confidence.

Others advanced useful models to show how knowledge gleaned from experience can produce personal change that in turn strengthens individuals aiming to effect organizational renewal. Scholars and practitioners have designed tools to systematically promote intentional change and therefore enhance leadership in organizations through a combination of real-world challenges, assessment, and social support (coaches who help extract meaningful lessons).[8]

Much has been learned about change in human systems from authors writing about the forces of resistance and the dynamics of organization culture. Organization theorists advanced the idea of "small wins" as a means for creating large-scale change.[9] Management gurus like Peter Drucker argued that "an innovation, to be effective, has to be simple and it has to be focused. Effective innovations start small."[10] More recently, managers have been exhorted to adopt an experimenter's scientific point of view, to equip themselves with the skills needed to engineer change.[11]

## Total Leadership in the Twenty-First Century

The Total Leadership program grows directly from these roots and responds to particular features of our present moment, the first years of a new millennium. The following sections briefly note the most critical.

### Social Change

The single-earner father and stay-at-home mother have been replaced by diverse models of "the standard home," demanding a radical revision in the expectations for time devoted to work, by men and women. Gender equity, while not yet achieved, is gaining ground in all spheres of society, creating new expectations and opportunities. In the wake of recent corporate scandals, the status of business is low, and citizens demand greater corporate accountability and ethical action. New public policies oblige business executives to find firmer moral ground and to avoid the temptations of greed.

### Demands of a New Workforce

People want to do work that has a positive impact on a world in which conflict seems pervasive. The best companies to work for are those in which employees work hard while having fun with people they see as their friends. Yet loyalty to a single organization is gone.

### Technological Shifts

The digital revolution is forcing everyone to learn how to exploit new communication tools that promise freedom (allowing us not to be bound to a particular time or place) but often lead to a new kind of slavery (24/7 connectivity). New media require that *we*—as leaders of our lives—choose where, when, and how to get things done, to manage the boundaries between different parts of life. This sets us apart from all prior generations, whose work routines were determined by the turning of the seasons and the rising and setting of the sun.

### Changes in Organizations and Markets

The torrid pace of change is compelling everyone in business to adapt to new situations, all the time. Ever-increasing demand for better productivity stresses and fragments our lives, causing health problems and burnout. At the same time, businesses are competing in the "war for talent" as labor shortages continue in critical sectors of the economy. Flatter organization structures mean a greater sense of responsibility for all, while globalization and the increasingly diverse pool of employees require new approaches to motivating people from different backgrounds.

## How to Use This Book

The Total Leadership program draws on these sources and responds to the demands of today's world. But it starts and ends with the individual, with *you*, in the context of your whole life and the relationships that matter most. Social structures and management practices shape the contours of what's possible in our everyday lives. The most powerful changes, though, are driven locally, by people who believe in themselves and who know how to get the support they need to make new things happen.

It takes leadership to drive change and make it so.

You've got to choose to lead, no matter what your position, no matter what the stage of your career, no matter what your life circumstances, no matter how much you are being buffeted by changing conditions. If you're going to make a difference, thinking of yourself as a leader will make it more likely that your legacy—not your fantasy, but the real impact of your life, today and in the long run—turns out to be the one you really want.

People are attracted to the Total Leadership method because they want to solve certain problems, but by going through its process, they usually discover solutions to problems they didn't even know they had. This book will take you through realistic steps so that you can become the leader you want to be.

The Total Leadership experience requires only that *you* take a realistic look at the big picture of your life and then use tools designed to help you lead more effectively. You'll decide on what changes you want to make and how you want to make them. You will be doing some serious introspection. But you'll also be reaching out to others. You'll have intensive, productive conversations with people in your inner circle. Because it involves other people, this program builds in accountability that makes changes stick.

While you may be tempted to skip around in the book, there is a well-honed logic to the process, and I encourage you to go through it in order, in its entirety. Take your time and be thoughtful about your responses to the assessments and exercises, as they set the stage for future actions.

If you are interested in a deeper exploration of the research under-lying the Total Leadership approach, appendix C, Further Reading, will familiarize you with the best relevant literature and research. And if you want tips on how to implement these ideas in a group or company, read appendix B, Scoring Four-Way Wins with Total Leadership in Your Organization.

### How to Use the Exercises

The exercises here will change how you think and act. I've tried to make the instructions straightforward so that you'll find them doable. Except in a few instances, I don't expect you to write things down in this book, so find a place to keep the things you write, whether it's in a hard-copy notebook or a digital file. You might even want to make audio or video recordings instead of literally writing.

The investment you're making in your growth as a leader takes time. A useful time frame for reading this book and doing the exercises—some of which will take place in minutes, others hours or days, and still others weeks—is about four months, start to finish. But you control the pace. This investment will be just the beginning of a new way for you to grow as a leader.

### How to Create a Coaching Network

While it is possible on your own to apply the basic principles of this book, you'll get more from it if you find companions in the process. Completing this program with others on your side is smart because it prevents your resolve from waning when no one's looking. Other people push you to do what you say you'll do, think more deeply, and see things differently to sustain real change. And you learn more by helping others with what they're trying to make happen.

Consider enlisting someone you know as your coach. A coach can provide another vantage point to help you refine what you learn through the early exercises, and then, later, to encourage intelligent risk taking in your experiments. A coach can help you to interpret your results, to crystallize the lessons you'll take away. He or she can also enhance your confidence by providing emotional support, and can give you specific ideas for achieving your goals.

The simplest approach is to find one other person to be both your coach and a client whom you'll coach. But better is to form a trio: a small network of friends, family, or colleagues. Let's say you've got Ali, Barb, and Charles. Ali coaches Barb, Barb coaches Charles, and Charles coaches Ali. This way, when you're coaching you're really focused on the other person, and vice versa. Coaching doesn't have to be complicated. It involves reading and commenting on what your client writes and talking with him about his actions. I'll let you know when, as a client, it's a good time to speak to your coach and, as a coach, to your client. I'll also give you suggestions for questions that will be useful for you to ask your client. See also appendix A, Your Total Leadership Coaching Network.

### *www.totalleadership.org*

You're not the only one wrestling with the challenges of becoming the leader you want to be and integrating work and the rest of life. I've created an online network to serve as a gathering point for a community of people dedicated to supporting each other's efforts to produce meaningful, sustainable change. At www.totalleadership.org you can have access to others who have taken the Total Leadership journey and who are eager to serve as coaches, share ideas, and promote innovation. You'll also find resources there, such as performance tools, further reading, interviews with thought leaders, examples of great experiments, stories about total leaders in action, and blogs and links on topics of interest.

## Getting Started: Your Goals

People who have gone through the Total Leadership program, like Jenna and André, report that they're living closer to the lives they want to lead, seeing their work as producing value not only for them but for others, and so they feel more connected and have a greater sense of purpose.

The Total Leadership process helps you develop your capacity for choosing the best direction. And while everyone takes the Total Leadership course for a different reason, most are eager for some sort of constructive change. Now, find a convenient place (notebook, electronic file, blog, audio or video recording—whatever suits you) to write briefly about your initial thoughts on why you're reading this book. Use the following exercise as a guide. Stating your goals explicitly will help you customize your experience throughout this book and will make it more likely that you reach them.

This initial exercise is both a starting point and a reference point. Assessing your goals establishes a baseline, which will make it easier to see how you've changed—how your performance has improved and

---

### YOUR GOALS FOR THE TOTAL LEADERSHIP PROGRAM

In a paragraph or two, describe what led you to read this book and what you hope to get out of it. Take a few moments to let your responses surface; then write your response in whatever place you've chosen to record your work for Total Leadership.

what you've learned about yourself as a leader—as a result of the work you will do throughout this book.

Yet your reasons for reading this book might shift over time. This happens often. Goals change. This is actually a good thing, because it shows that you're thinking about what's important and that you're adapting as new opportunities arise and as you see things from new points of view.

Now let's move on to learning about what it means to be real.

# PART I

# BE REAL
## Act with Authenticity

## CHAPTER 2

# Clarify What's Important to You

THE ESSENCE OF BEING REAL, of acting with authenticity, is in knowing what you care about and then doing your best to be true to these values and aspirations. The exercises you'll do in this chapter will help you articulate these most important aspects of your life's purpose, and so provide the foundation for everything else you'll do in the rest of this book.

You can't help but like Kerry Tanaka right from the start. She works in marketing for a pharmaceutical company, for which she travels a lot, especially to Europe. At twenty-seven, she's single and keeps her five-foot-four-inch frame fit by running in marathons. Kerry is a first-generation American, born in the United States to parents who were both from Japan. "Growing up as a Japanese American in an upper-middle-class, white community—looking different on the outside—forced me to focus on shaping the type of person that I am on the inside," she said. She lives alone in the pastel-colored condo she bought recently in San Francisco.

Her perky enthusiasm for everything she does makes her a real pleasure to be around.

When I asked Kerry, at the beginning of her Total Leadership journey, to describe in the best case what her future would look like, fifteen years hence, she wrote:

Fifteen years from now, I look back with some amazement on the growth of the ten-year-old company I am running, having overseen its expansion from seventeen people at the start to the nearly one thousand employees today. The executive team has fostered a culture of belonging. People feel like part of a family, and all employees know their contributions to the bottom line are essential. They look forward to coming to work each day and are committed not only to the products we are developing and marketing, but also to the people they work with. We are proud of our portfolio of innovative products, which makes a real difference to the physicians who prescribe them and the patients who use them.

People see me as a leader with integrity, humility, and compassion. They know I don't forget my roots. I remember my employees' names and know them as people, not just as workers. I know their families and they know me. Many women think of me as their mentor. I recognize the potential and abilities of the future stars of my company and care about cultivating the next generation of leaders.

I have a family of my own. My kids are in grade school. I have the type of relationship with them that I have had with my mom. I am involved in their lives—going on field trips, supporting them in their extracurricular activities, and being a friend, teacher, disciplinarian, and caregiver. My kids are growing up to be kind, compassionate adults. Helping to make this happen is the most important thing I've done.

Let me take you back from Kerry's imagined future to the present. Kerry typically puts in an eleven-hour day. Her hectic travel schedule doesn't get her to where she would most like to go: to see her parents and brother. They live far away; she misses them. She makes up for the absence of family, in part, with her diverse circle of friends, a few very close ones and many casual ones. Outgoing and social, Kerry loves to join her boyfriend and other friends for dinner, movies, and concerts. Yet, despite all of her activities, something's missing.

When I asked her to say why she wanted to try the Total Leadership program, Kerry answered that "being a single woman, I tend to focus like a laser on work and professional development. Ultimately, this has left me feeling empty. I want to make time for my close friends, so we can just have fun and chat about the things that are important in our lives. People at work are fairly supportive, but I don't think they understand my desire to better sync my home life with my life at work."

You just read excerpts from Kerry's responses to some of the exercises in this chapter, all of which are designed to help you to pay attention to yourself and your world—to see things in a new light. Clarifying what's important lets you identify gaps between what you value, how you're acting in your life, and how you are interacting with the people who matter most to you. This then enables you to imagine meaningful change.

By the end of this chapter, you'll have done some introspection about your life's important events, your heroes, your desired future, and your core values. All told, these exercises should take about three hours. (Some people spend more time and some less; you certainly don't have to do it all in one sitting.) My main advice is to take the time—don't rush it—and be honest with yourself. You'll get the most out of this important foundation building if you write openly and candidly. Keep in mind that the versions you produce in these exercises, for your own private use, need not be the same as the versions you might choose to show others.

## Where Have You Come From?

To deepen your awareness—of who you are and who you want to be—look back and assess what events and people have shaped you, and then write about them. You are addressing big questions here: Who am I? Where do I come from? Doing this will make it easier and more meaningful, in the following exercises, to write about where you're going and what you care about most. And this, in turn, makes it easier for you to talk about these things in a comfortable and engaging way with the people who matter most.

## WHERE HAVE YOU COME FROM?

For this exercise, find a comfortable place to reflect, and then compose your responses—in a journal, in a blog, on an audiotape, or anywhere—to the two questions below. Give yourself ample time to do both, in one sitting or in multiple sittings.

### Your Story: Critical Events in Your Life

Think back over your personal history and identify the four or five most important events or episodes in your life, the moments that have defined who you are today. Tell the story of these events, in chronological order, and for each one, briefly describe the impact the event had on your values and on your direction in life.

### Your Hero: Someone You Admire

In a paragraph or so, describe someone you admire. Think of this person as someone you see as heroic in an important way. It might be someone whom you know personally or someone you only know about but have never met. After you describe him or her, write a sentence or two about what makes this person admirable to you.

To convey a story that inspires others, you have to find a way, somehow, to make sense of your personal history and then connect it to the collective—whether that collective means people at work, your family, or friends and community members. Thinking through these connections starts with the events that have influenced the ideals you hold most dear.

Martin Luther King Jr. wove the strands of *his* own life into our collective history and passionately communicated an image of what an entire nation could achieve in his "I have a dream" speech—a call to action in 1963 that moved a generation of Americans to produce lasting change. It's the best example I know of the power that comes from connecting a personal story with a collective narrative. When, at the start of that speech, he recounted the litany of historical injustices, we knew he had suffered them personally. And when he spoke about the future, it was his vision for *his* family, but also for *our* country: "I have a dream that my four little children will one day live in a nation where they will not be judged by the color of their skin but by the content of their character." None of us can be King, of course, but we can all emulate him, in our own way, because we all have the capacity to relate our own story to the larger one of which we're a part.

I really do mean for you to tell a story. "The story is a basic human cognitive form," writes Howard Gardner in *Leading Minds*. "The artful creation and articulation of stories constitutes a fundamental part of the leader's vocation." Gardner adds, "Narratives that help individuals think about and feel who they are, where they come from, and where they are headed . . . constitute the single most powerful weapon in the leader's literary arsenal."[1]

When you tell your leadership story, you articulate your "defining moments," as leadership scholar Joseph Badaracco calls them. They often involve choices you've made in your life in which your values are revealed, shaped, and put to the test. These episodes create clarity about the things that matter to you, about your abiding commitments. Steve Jobs, cofounder of Apple, spoke at Stanford University's graduation in

2005 and told a story about when he was fired at thirty years old from the company he'd created in his parents' garage ten years earlier:

> It was a very public failure, and I even thought about running away from the Valley. But something slowly began to dawn on me—I still loved what I did. The turn of events at Apple had not changed that one bit. I had been rejected, but I was still in love. And so I decided to start over.
>
> I didn't see it then, but it turned out that getting fired from Apple was the best thing that could have ever happened to me. The heaviness of being successful was replaced by the lightness of being a beginner again, less sure about everything. It freed me to enter one of the most creative periods of my life.[2]

Jobs told this story to teach a lesson, to illustrate the importance of staying true to yourself, of authenticity, and choosing to pursue work that is meaningful. His story speaks volumes about persisting in the face of rejection to find the freedom to be the leader you want to be.

> I'm convinced that the only thing that kept me going was that I loved what I did. You've got to find what you love. And that is as true for your work as it is for your lovers. Your work is going to fill a large part of your life, and the only way to be truly satisfied is to do what you believe is great work. And the only way to do great work is to love what you do. If you haven't found it yet, keep looking. Don't settle.

### Roxanne's Story

When you meet Roxanne Pappas-Grant in a work situation, you are struck by her focus and the degree to which she is in control, and takes control, of any situation. In her early forties, she has well-coiffed hair, perfect teeth, and subtle makeup that enhance the natural beauty of her soft eyes and nose. She's every inch the consummate business manager of the twenty-first century: strongly driven to succeed, Roxanne is an engineer heading up sales development for a division of a multinational chemical company. "I have always been incredibly focused on my career," she said about herself, "and on accomplishment through career progression."

Roxanne, though, has another side. She's also a wife and mother who, when I first met her, had been growing less and less satisfied with her life as she felt increasingly disconnected from her family, especially her children. Work is really important to Roxanne, but it's not everything: "I have learned through hardship that my career accomplishments do not define who I am, and I've discovered that I have a lot to offer in ways that are not always rewarded in the work world." When asked about her goals for Total Leadership, she said, "I believe that I should have a clearer vision of what I want to accomplish in my life, not only in my work life, and uncover what constitutes success in this arena. It is this journey to uncover what is most important to me—I am not sure I yet know—that has led me here."

Early in her Total Leadership experience, Roxanne came to see that the person she is at work—the values and interests she pursues in that area of her life—is not the person she wants to be outside of work. This disappointed her, and she looked to find ways to be her true self at work to build her relationship with her children, which would also enhance her sense of self and, she hoped, make her more effective in her career.

To begin the process of redefining her work persona, Roxanne wrote about the critical events in her life:

My father has had a strong impact on my life. He has very high standards for performance, believes there is no substitute for hard work, and believes one should always look inward to discover how to improve. My birth was his last chance for a son—there was even a boy's name picked out for me. Instead of being disappointed, he decided I would be "the son he never had" by transferring a lot of his own hopes and dreams to me. He came to the United States as an immigrant from Greece and trained as an electrician's apprentice. He guided me to become an electrical engineer, to learn how to think and to have more opportunity than he had.

In school, I wasn't one of the popular kids, and I studied more than socialized. I found it liberating not to be part of the "cool crowd." I could take actions that I thought were more principled; I didn't have to concern myself with what my friends would think or do. This led me to value being respected over being liked—a value I've found important as a leader. I must admit, though, that it's nice to be liked.

In college, I did become a "popular kid." While I still valued being respected over being liked, I discovered that I had a knack for motivating people. In my senior year, I was president of four campus organizations and very active in four others. I found that I had a genuine desire to work with people, and although I was strongly pursued by the engineering school for the doctoral program in electrical engineering, I opted for a role in managing people and teams.

Writing about critical events in her life helped Roxanne see more clearly how she came to be who she is and what matters to her. For one thing, it reinforced her sense of being on the right track in her career. And it helped her to understand why she tends to focus on work in a way that detracts from achieving other important goals in her life.

Everyone has a story to tell, and each one is different. Everyone's leadership journey is, and must be, a unique one. Further, the more you're able to draw on the actual story of your life, and tell it, when you're trying to convey what's important to you and where you're headed, the more the people around you will know, understand, and relate well to you.

I urge you to practice so that you can become a good storyteller. Learn to tell inspiring stories about who you are and where you are going. As Noel Tichy explains in his classic, *The Leadership Engine*, "The most effective leaders are those who are in touch with their leadership stories . . . When we know our stories, we know ourselves." Your stories, though, are not just for you. They are important because, as Tichy writes, "they allow other people to know us. Stories create real, human connections by allowing others to get inside our minds and our lives."[3]

### Heroes of Kerry and André

It's also useful to explore the people you have admired and their stories. Describing a hero of yours and explaining what you admire about him or her helps you visualize a real person who embodies qualities you'd like to emulate. It's another window on the leader you want to become. Kerry chose as her hero her younger brother, Dan.

At the age of twenty-four, Dan enlisted in the U.S. Army. Throughout his tour of duty, he has shown incredible resolve and discipline. Since enlisting, he has been completely focused on two things: finishing up his college degree and becoming a Green Beret. He is well on the way to accomplishing both goals. After researching the details of the strenuous Green Beret/Special Forces qualifying course, he trained for several months to prepare himself both physically and mentally. Dan was selected and begins his Green Beret/Combat Medic training in three weeks. I have no doubt that he will successfully complete the rigorous two-year training program. Dan is my hero because he has relentlessly pursued his objectives. But more importantly, I have a great deal of respect for how he has pursued them. He has demonstrated character and passion throughout.

Kerry's choice reflects not only the importance of her brother to her, but the value of perseverance, pursuing goals that matter, and doing so in a way that generates respect. Describing her brother as her hero led her to see more clearly that these are important values for her own life.

André Washington chose his mother as his hero.

> She was born in the segregated South, and is the third of ten children. Her mother died from a respiratory illness resulting from poor working conditions, and at the age of sixteen my mother moved to Chicago, where she was then raised by her aunt. After marrying my father and moving west—and after suffering several years of spousal abuse—she divorced him and found herself alone raising two children. Over the next several years, working for wages below the poverty line, she successfully sent her two children to college and, following their graduation, earned her own BA in social work. All personal, professional, and spiritual growth I have achieved over my lifetime I owe to the selfless dedication and determination of my mother. Her life continues to inspire my every motivation to achieve.

André sees his mother as a model for how to persevere in the face of adversity. Reflecting on people you admire taps into strong emotions, because people we admire usually demonstrate a dramatic triumph of resolve over harsh realities. Everyone can relate to this kind of struggle and, in itself, it's useful as a reminder that the achievements of most leaders—people who aim to change things, to make things better—are hard won.

Telling the story of people who matter to you, and why they matter, is also a powerful means for conveying your values to others. It's a way of revealing things about yourself in an authentic way—in a way to which others can easily relate. You'll see just how useful this is as we move along in the Total Leadership process, when you talk with the people closest to you about what's most important to you.

## Your Leadership Vision

The next step in clarifying what's important is to write what I'll refer to as your *leadership vision*—a *compelling image* of an *achievable future*. It is an essential means for focusing your attention on what matters most to you—what you want to accomplish in your life and what kind of leader you wish to become. A useful leadership vision must be rooted in your past and address the future while dealing with today's realities. It represents who you are and what you stand for, and it inspires you, and the people whose commitment you need, to act to make constructive change toward a future you all want to see.

It's important that this story of the future you're inventing is indeed a compelling image of an achievable future. Let's examine each of the four key words.

- A *compelling* story of the future is engaging; it captures the heart, forces you to pay attention. Those who hear it want to be a part of it somehow. And they are moved. Think of King's stirring language and the ideas –freedom and justice—that appeal to our highest aspirations.

- And if others could travel into the future with you, what would they find? What does your future look like—what's the *image*? A well-crafted leadership vision is described in concrete terms that are easy to visualize and remember. Think of King again: "One day right there in Alabama little black boys and black girls will be able to join hands with little white boys and white girls as sisters and brothers." Everyone can picture that and know what it means.

- Your vision, the story of your future, should be a stretch, but it must be *achievable*, too. If it were not achievable, you would have little motivation to even bother trying. Again, King: "With this faith, we will be able to work together, to pray together, to struggle together, to go to jail together, to stand up for freedom together, knowing that we will be free one day." It's not a pie in the sky. It is possible.

- Finally, *future* simply means out there—some time from this moment forward, but not so far away that's it's out of reach. In his sensational conclusion, King calls for sounding the chimes of freedom *now* so that a new, changed world arrives, faster: "When we let it ring from every village and every hamlet, from every state and every city, we will be able to speed up that day."

While you may want to write the story of your future in the form of a detailed plan that charts specific milestones for the road ahead, don't get so hung up on particular targets that if you fail to hit them, you'll be disappointed. This isn't meant to be an exercise in project management but, rather, an opportunity for you to dream, with your head in the clouds *and* your feet on the ground. So, while you should say a few things about how you've gotten to where you are fifteen years hence—the journey, that is—write as much in this story about the destination, what your everyday life actually looks like once you're there.

Also, understand that inspiration is a function of great aspirations. What contributions to our world do you dream of making? Try to focus part of what you compose on how you will, in the future, be making the world a better place in some way, for other people. You might think of this as your legacy. If, in other words, fifteen years more is all you have, what you will leave behind after you're gone? What will your life have meant to others?

Like all the exercises here in this first part of the book, describing your leadership vision in writing raises your awareness of what is important to you. It will likely give you new ideas for what you might do to better align your actions with your values. It should provide inspiration

## YOUR LEADERSHIP VISION

In this exercise, describe the kind of leader you want to become by writing a short story of your life between now and fifteen years in the future.

Take your time to think about it and start writing as soon as you're ready. Write vividly. Make it come alive and don't hold back. The more of yourself you can pour into this, the more valuable it will be to you as you progress through this book.

What if you don't even know where you want to go with your life or what you want it to look like? Give it your best shot. Open your mind to your imagination, and try not to be constrained by what you think others want and need from you. (In the next part of the book, we'll deal with the expectations of others.) Take the leap.

Ideally, your finished draft will be about one page. It will be a compelling image of an achievable future. It will also describe the journey, how you got there, and the destination, what a typical day looks like. Finally, it will show how you're making the world better in some way.

for the choices you're making now—and in the long run—about how to spend your precious time.

It's natural to have some trepidation about writing the story of your future. (In fact, it's natural to have some anxiety about many of the exercises in the Total Leadership process.) There are risks involved when you articulate your leadership vision: what if it doesn't come true? Another possibly inhibiting thought is what others might make of it. How much of what's inside—your goals and aspirations—can you trust other people to respect? Don't worry about that for now. I'll get to the subject of how to communicate your vision to others after you've written your first draft. Remember that throughout this whole process, you control your information, and you need not reveal anything to anyone if you don't want to.

Some people find it difficult to write a story about the future because they do not want to make the choices it requires. A leader chooses goals, after all, a purpose that establishes something to aim for and move toward, even if it's only to help focus on what matters most right now. The aim of doing this exercise here, at the start, is to build your foundation: a story of your future is a point of departure and, as you'll see later, a point of return.

This leadership vision is not fixed or immutable. You will adjust it as you change and as things change around you. New information, new opportunities, new obstacles will compel you to revise it. And when you put the story of your future out there for others to comment on it, you might hear some things you don't want to hear. People might say you can't do it or that it's foolish. But if you don't let others know about it, then the likelihood of achieving it is reduced.

The more genuine your story of your future and the more people that know it, the more others will want, and know how, to contribute to making it come true, even if they may not value it now. A real leadership challenge is to show how *your* vision is the one that *others* also want, need, and will find real value in. Indeed, what is the essence of leadership if not in finding creative ways of describing a vision that others see as what they are trying to achieve?

### Victor's Leadership Vision

Victor Gardner wrote the story of his future when he was in his midthirties. A classic Englishman, Victor is reserved and inscrutable, with a wry sense of humor. His wire-rimmed glasses and sharply parted blond hair give him an air of thoughtful authority, befitting his role as director of an information technology unit in a major investment bank in New York, where he resides with his wife and two children—a six-year-old boy and three-year-old daughter.

Victor's job involves important responsibilities: he comanages a group that is building a new trading software system, he coordinates the interactions of this group with users at the executive level, and he is responsible for driving this team of twenty high-performing engineers while nurturing their careers. Yet he doesn't always feel stretched. He yearns to do something that allows him to "be able to build new things—computer systems, houses, companies, anything." Further, he wants to feel that his work is "making a meaningful difference to something or someone." He wants to "spark the passion" he once felt.

Some of Victor's leadership vision appears below. This was his first draft, less important as a model of what a "good" leadership vision *should* be, than an illustration of what it *might* be.

Fifteen years ago, I turned the corner in my working life. I climbed out of my "going through the motions" rut and rediscovered what I liked about working in technology. I also managed to crack the code of how to inspire people by making them feel good about themselves and the work they were doing. I actually learned this by working with my kids, teaching them to read and to play their first musical instruments.

The team was very successful, and its software went on to become my company's dominant desktop platform . . . [Its success] gave me freedom to focus on working in a more entrepreneurial way within the bank, building and delivering systems for many of our new business ventures . . .

I continued to work at the bank for the next five years, but I was able to embark on a couple of side ventures with colleagues and friends. In one I was able to leverage my interest in real estate to put together a syndicate that purchased an old warehouse building, renovated it, and turned it into upscale residential apartments. Each member of my family was involved in these ventures, and this was one of the ways in which I managed to teach the kids that they could do pretty much anything that they choose to, if they set their mind to it.

I finally moved from the large corporate world to a smaller entrepreneurial situation. I had been tinkering with some artificial intelligence applications and had built a prototype of software I believed had real market value. I set up shop with a small group of people who had complementary skills, and we built a company that revolutionized how new technology is constructed.

A couple of years ago, I felt that it was time to step aside from day-to-day operations. I love gardening and began overseeing restoration projects in my local park. I also started fund-raising efforts for local botanical gardens.

Victor's leadership vision says a lot about what mattered to him at the time he wrote it. And it shows that he was beginning to see new ways of applying resources gained from his experiences in one life domain (teaching his children) to get things done in another (inspiring his employees). Writing the story of his future transformation—from working in a senior managerial position at a large bank to being his own boss, working with friends in non-bank-like settings—helped propel him faster in that direction. In reflecting about it afterward, he began to see that the task of integrating the domains of his life is an ongoing challenge and that he need not wait until he's retired to do the things he enjoys in life. And he came to see new meaning in, and opportunities for, contributions to community and society. Most importantly, writing his vision, and then talking about it, encouraged Victor to make constructive changes in the present.

When it comes to communicating your leadership vision, you've got to have some passion. And when you paint an image of the future for others to see, you want your excitement to be contagious. It takes practice to do this in a way that is natural for you. And you will get better at it, if you try, even if you're not a gifted speaker.

The source of passion about the future you're creating is in your past. The trick is to tap into feelings about the past, which people spontaneously do when they talk about the most meaningful incidents in their lives. When you tell the story of your future, to yourself and to others, it's useful to include a story from your real past. Doing so makes the story of your future authentic, grounded as it is in the truth of your own real experience.

The answer to a common question, "What if I don't feel passionate about my career?" is to think back on our lives and focus on what has been most meaningful—and, preferably, enjoyable—so far. This leads to fruitful ideas about how to create a future in which talents and passions find outlets.

As a leader in all areas of life, you've got to look back in order to move forward.

## Your Core Values

Just as every organization has its own unique set of values, so does every person. Your values—what you hold most dear and are willing to strive or even fight for—determine your actions as a leader and how you view the world around you. In order to act in a way that is consistent with your values—to be authentic, that is—you have to be conscious of what those values are. You'll describe yours in this next exercise, which can be done quickly but merits enough time to be done completely.

## YOUR CORE VALUES

On one page, list the values (between five and nine is ideal) that are most important to you. For each one, explain why it's important to you in one or two sentences. To spur your thinking, here is a list of values excerpted from Robert Lee and Sara King's *Discovering the Leader in You*.[a] Of course, you may choose terms that don't appear on this list.

Achievement:  a sense of accomplishment or mastery

Advancement:  growth, seniority, and promotion resulting from work well done

Adventure:  new and challenging opportunities, excitement, risk

Aesthetics:  appreciation of beauty in things, ideas, surroundings

Affiliation:  interaction with other people, recognition as a member of a group, belonging

Affluence:  high income, financial success, prosperity

Authority:  position and power to control events and other people's activities

Autonomy:  ability to act independently with few constraints, self-reliance

Challenge:  continually facing complex and demanding tasks and problems

Change and variation:  absence of routine, unpredictability

Collaboration:  close, cooperative working relationships with groups

Community:  serving and supporting a purpose that supersedes personal desires

Competency:  demonstrating high proficiency and knowledge

**Competition:** rivalry with winning as the goal

**Courage:** willingness to stand up for beliefs

**Creativity:** discovering, developing, or designing new ideas or things; demonstrating imagination

**Diverse perspectives:** unusual ideas and opinions that may not seem right or be popular at first

**Duty:** respect for authority, rules, and regulations

**Economic security:** steady and secure employment, adequate reward, low risk

**Enjoyment:** fun, joy, and laughter

**Family:** spending time with partner, children, parents, extended family

**Friendship:** close personal relationships with others

**Health:** physical and mental well-being, vitality

**Helping others:** helping people attain their goals, providing care and support

**Humor:** the ability to laugh at myself and at life

**Influence:** having an impact on attitudes or opinions of others

**Inner harmony:** happiness, contentment, being at peace with yourself

**Justice:** fairness, doing the right thing

**Knowledge:** the pursuit of understanding, skill, and expertise; continual learning

**Location:** choice of a place to live that is conducive to a desired lifestyle

**Love:** involvement in close, affectionate relationships; intimacy

**Loyalty:** faithfulness; dedication to individuals, traditions, or organizations

**Order:** stability, routine, predictability, clear lines of authority, standardization

**Personal development:** dedication to maximizing potential

**Physical fitness:** staying in shape through physical activity and healthy nutrition

**Recognition:** positive feedback and public credit for work well done; respect and admiration

**Responsibility:** dependability, accountability for results

**Self-respect:** pride, self-esteem, sense of knowing oneself

**Spirituality:** strong spiritual or religious beliefs, moral fulfillment

**Status:** being respected for a job or an association with a prestigious group or organization

**Trustworthiness:** being known as reliable and sincere

**Wisdom:** sound judgment based on knowledge, experience, and understanding

a. Adapted from Robert J. Lee and Sara N. King, *Discovering the Leader in You* (San Francisco: Jossey-Bass, 2001), 60–61. Reprinted with permission of John Wiley & Sons, Inc.

Most people don't change their values during the course of the Total Leadership program. Core values spring, indeed, from your *core*—they are usually long-standing and resistant to change. Like all the work you've done so far in this chapter, what you just wrote is a unique list, particular to your constitution, background, and experience.

I'm sure it's different from Victor's. Here's the list of his most important values, with his reason for each entry.

**Authenticity**—I must believe in what I am doing. Without that, people can see the lack of passion, and leadership becomes ineffective.

**Honesty and trust**—With honesty comes trust, and without trust, the only effective leadership style is coercion. Conversely, I think it's also important to trust others: to get their job done, to do the right thing.

**Inspiration**—The most effective leaders can make people feel that they want to show up every day and give it their best shot. They make people feel good about who they are and the work that they are doing. They inspire the best out of people.

**Respect and being respected**—It is important to respect others, from all walks of life. Everyone has something worthy of respect; it's important to find that.

**Courage**—Too many leaders avoid the hard questions, avoid the groundbreaking moves. Courage and the willingness to be wrong is a must-have.

**Family**—Work is work, but your family is your life. When all is said and done, my wife and kids are the most important things to me. Apparently, this is not a credo I live by every minute of every day, but when the chips are down, they are the most important.

Your distinctive values are an important part of what will make your own particular brand of leader. At this point it's useful to think about how your everyday life squares with what you said was important to you here, and what you might try to do that would result in a better fit than currently exists.

## Pause and Reflect

Having completed the exercises so far, you have taken important steps in building your leadership capacity, improving your performance, and integrating the different parts of your life. You've spent time clarifying your motivations for reading this book, depicting important events in your life and their meaning to you, characterizing someone you've admired and what you've learned from him or her, inventing a story of your desired future, and identifying your core values.

You've become familiar with terms that might be new for you and that I'll be using the rest of the way—like leadership vision—and you may have started to think about things you can do now to make changes that will strengthen your sense of yourself as a leader who acts with authenticity, integrity, and creativity. Jot down any such ideas as they're percolating. Some people find it useful to keep a file, "Ideas for Action," that will become especially useful when you're designing your experiments.

You've met others who, each starting from a different place, have taken a journey of their own. (You'll meet the rest of the group in coming chapters.) You might think of these fellow travelers as making up a virtual learning community. They are people from whom you can learn by comparing your thoughts and reactions with theirs.

And if you're working on Total Leadership with people you know—with a coaching trio or with another person—now is a good time to speak with them about what you've been thinking and writing. Ideally, you'll have two conversations. First, find a mutually convenient time, about an hour, to review the material you've produced in this chapter with your coach. Then find another time to serve as a coach for someone else who's just completed the exercises so far. Appendix A is a guide for how to get the most out of your Total Leadership experience through serving as both a coach and a client.

## PAUSE AND REFLECT ON
## WHAT'S IMPORTANT

Whether you pause and reflect on your own or supplement your thinking with coaching conversations, in person or online at www.totalleadership.org, here are things to keep in mind as you synthesize what you've done in chapter 2 before moving on to chapter 3.

Read through your responses to the previous exercises in this chapter. Consider the following questions. Write about them and then, if possible, talk about them with your coach.

1. What are the main ideas you take away from what you've just read?

2. Tell the story of your critical events and your leadership vision to someone. What do you learn from how they react?

3. What are the main connections between your past and your vision for the future?

4. What changes might you make to live more closely in accord with what really matters to you?

## CHAPTER 3

# Take the Four-Way View

NOW THAT YOU'VE thought about your core values and your vision of the kind of world you want to create, we're ready to go deeper into what it means for you to act with authenticity by exploring the relative importance of the four domains of your life, the attention you give them, whether the goals you pursue in each one are in sync with the others, and how satisfied you are with how things are going, in each area and altogether. Like Kerry, Lim Chang did all this too.

Lim's five-foot-ten-inch body barely contains his infectious energy. His jet-black hair contrasts sharply with the pearly-white teeth that shine brightly through his smile. Lim is the "rah-rah" guy on the soccer team who is always screaming to pump up his teammates. The son of a physician father and a homemaker mother, Lim, thirty-four, and his wife have a two-year-old son and another on the way. From offices in Orange County, he and the dozen people directly reporting to him manage West Coast operations of a national retail design firm. Although he works fifty-five to sixty hours each week, he makes it a point not to work on weekends.

He runs marathons for fun, though when I first met him, Lim was finding it quite difficult to keep up his exercise regimen. The issues that motivated his interest in my Total Leadership course were not unlike those many people confront. He was having a hard time achieving what at first he called "balance" between the different areas of his life. Here's what he wrote about his early efforts in the program, about two years after having completed it:

One of the exercises in the initial push to clarify what was important was a chart that showed the level of importance of each of my four life domains and the time I was devoting to each. It became clear that I was paying a disproportionate amount of attention to my career and that I wasn't spending nearly enough time on developing my mind, body, and spirit.

But it wasn't just about how I was spending my time, as I saw when I drew four circles representing what I really cared about in each of the four domains. I asked myself, did the circles line up as they do in the center of a tree, or were they disconnected, like random puddles all over the place? Was I being the person (the strong, centered "tree") I really wanted to be? The short answer: no. This made me feel uncomfortable.

I rated how happy I was with the different aspects of my life, and I was surprised. If someone had simply asked me how satisfied I was in each domain, the answers would not have matched that chart. By assessing the importance, time, and energy I gave to each domain, and the give-and-take among them, I was able to more realistically evaluate my overall satisfaction. It turned out that I was much more satisfied with work and family than with my community and self—that was not my intuition going into the exercise.

I started asking . . . What changes could I make to pay more attention to what really mattered to me—and less to what didn't?

What was it that I was doing at work and at home that made me feel good about how things were going there? Was it that my behavior at work and at home was more consistent with my core values? What would people at work and home say made me most successful? If I could answer these questions, I might find new ways of using what I already knew about producing satisfaction at work and at home to improve my community and self areas.

Just as Lim did, in this chapter you're going to learn to take the four-way view. By looking closely at the different domains of your life—work, home, community, and self—you'll clarify what's important to you and see your life from a fresh perspective. You'll also begin to explore what it means for you to act with integrity by recognizing the whole person.

The exercises you'll do in this chapter will help you to discover whether you're being real: are you paying attention to what you care about most, acting in ways that are consistent with the person you want to be, going after goals that matter, and achieving happiness in all the parts as well in your life as a whole?

## Define Your Domains

Start by defining your four domains. This is a subjective process, so you must define your domains in whatever way makes the most sense for you. For most people, the work domain is your job: what you do for a living or, if you're between jobs, what you're aiming to do next. If you're in school, whether or not you have a job as well, then school is part of your work domain. To fully grasp what your work domain comprises, think beyond just the hours you sit in your cubicle, office, or whatever your work space is, and consider the wide array of things you do as part of your career. This might include taking classes, traveling, participating in trade associations, talking to mentors about your career, or doing research on future entrepreneurial opportunities.

Then there's the home, or family, domain. Again, it's a subjective judgment you'll make here. This domain can include the people (or animals) you live with, your family of origin (parents, siblings, and others), or your family of creation (spouse, significant other, children, and others).

Likewise, the net you cast around your community or society domain can be as wide as you like, including friends, neighbors, social groups, religious institutions, charitable activities, political committees, membership in nonprofit organizations, or anything that bears on your impact on the world beyond your work and your family.

Finally, there is the domain of your self. This includes your emotional health, intellectual knowledge, physical health, leisure, and spiritual life.

## The Four-Way Attention Chart

The next step in understanding your four life domains is to examine your choices about the focus of your attention to them in light of their relative importance to you. Completing the four-way attention chart fills in an essential part of the picture of how things stand today. It shows how you manage the allocation of your time and energy—the amount of attention you pay to the various people and projects in your life—and so helps you assess whether you're actually doing what you care about doing.

This chart doesn't, however, address the other part of the picture: whether or not your actions and your goals for each domain—the how and the why—are in harmony with the others. We'll explore that later in this chapter. Together, these two assessments give a full picture of whether you're demonstrating authenticity and being real in all domains of your life. And painting it is a crucial step forward in your thinking about the experiments you might try to improve your satisfaction and performance in all domains.

Keep in mind, as you do this exercise, that your subjective judgment is all that matters here. For instance, your involvement in community and society is whatever this means to you, and not what others want of you. So it may be about giving money to charity, helping your friends, cleaning up your neighborhood, or getting involved in targeted campaigns to make the world a better place. And remember that this chart indicates only how you see things now. When you complete this chart again, after your experiments, your numbers will probably be different, if you're like most people who've done this. As you progress through the book— as you learn more about how to demonstrate authenticity, integrity, and creativity—the relationships among work, home, community, and self will change.

## THE FOUR-WAY ATTENTION CHART

One way of being real is to grasp the connection between the importance of each part of your life and what you actually pay attention to every day. The chart below is another window through which to see what's important to you. In the first column, consider the relative importance of each major area of your life today. Assign a percentage to each and make sure they add up to 100. If you place as much importance on work/career/school as you do on the other three areas of your life combined, put "50%" in that cell on the chart. If, as another example, all four domains are of equal importance to you, then put "25%" in each cell of the first column.

In the second column, consider how much time and energy you actually focus on each domain in a typical week. Assign a percentage to each. Make sure these numbers, too, add up to 100.

| Domain | Importance | Focus of time and energy |
|---|---|---|
| Work/Career/School | % | % |
| Home/Family | % | % |
| Community/Society | % | % |
| Self: mind, body, spirit | % | % |
| | 100% | 100% |

After you've completed the chart, write notes in response to the following questions:

1. What are the consequences of the current choices you make about your focus of time and energy spent at work, at home, in the community, and for yourself?

2. As you look at these eight numbers, are there any adjustments you'd like to make—either in what's important or in where you focus your attention—to change any of these numbers?

3. What would it take to actually make these adjustments in your life?

## Victor's Four-Way Attention Chart

Victor assessed the importance of the four major areas of his life by assigning these percentages in the first column: 35, 35, 10, and 20. At the time he started the Total Leadership program, Victor's work domain included being an IT director in a major bank *and* being a student in a full-time executive MBA program that convened for classes every other weekend and for longer stretches in the summer. This part, he observed, was equal in weight to his family domain, which comprised his wife, two children, and parents. His community domain, he noted, comprised a few friends and just a bit more. Of the four domains, he was unapologetic about this being the least important to him. Finally, his interest in his own personal fulfillment was less important to him than his work and his family, but more important than his involvement in community and society.

Victor then distributed percentages to indicate how much time and energy he actually spent in each area, in a typical week, in the second column: 65, 20, 5, and 10. In a demonstration of an obvious mismatch— which most people report when they do this exercise—he overemphasized work compared with the other domains. Everyone's chart is unique, of course. But what typically transpires over the course of the Total Leadership program is a noticeable move toward a closer fit between what's important and where you devote your attention. Here's some of what Victor said about his four-way attention chart:

What I care about and what I do with my time are not very well aligned. The mismatch with my family really bothers me. I make an effort to spend time at either end of the day to be around our kids by taking them to school, or just trying to get home before they go to bed, but our interactions aren't going that well at the moment— probably because I'm so preoccupied with work and school. My wife's started to refer to herself as a "single mom."

I just don't care much about my community domain right now. I try to keep up with my friends and do a small amount of volunteering and charitable giving. It's all I can do. And as for my self domain, I'm probably in the worst physical and spiritual shape ever. But I feel that I need to defer doing anything about this right now.

I'm just trying to do everything—and succeeding at little. It's imperative that I find ways of having the different parts of my life create more positive impact on each other. Otherwise, I don't see how I can keep dissatisfaction in one area of my life from spilling over into other areas.

The self-awareness Victor developed through this exercise was an important step. By thinking about his responses to his four-way attention chart, Victor started asking new questions about where he might find opportunities for constructive change in how he wove together his work and the rest of his life. Was there a way, for example, for him to make adjustments that would make his wife feel less like a "single mom" that would, at the same time, inspire him to bring greater enthusiasm to his work? Was it possible for him to give more attention to improving his physical well-being and, in doing so, produce benefits not only for his health but also for his employer, his family, and his community?

These questions helped him to start thinking about some changes. But there was more to do still in finding gaps between the current state of things and what he really wanted in his life.

## Your Four Circles

Once you have completed your four-way attention chart, you're ready to draw a graphical representation of the four domains that will help you perceive whether or not they are in harmony. The attention chart is especially useful for getting you to look squarely at the issue of your choices about the allocation of your attention—your time and energy. Drawing the four circles asks you to consider a different question: are you the same person wherever you go?

Here, it's not a matter of how much attention you're devoting to the different parts of your life but, rather, how the interests you are serving in one domain relate to your interests in the other domains. Are you being the person you want to be, no matter where you are in life?

We'll use your four circles as another tool for gaining a deeper understanding of what's important to you in the different roles you play in life, how they affect each other, and where there are gaps between domains that you can close.

## THE FOUR CIRCLES

Are the four domains of your life compatible or in conflict? Before you draw anything, there are two choices to make as you think about the pattern of your four circles.

- **Consider size.** The first choice you've already made; that is, the *size* of the circles. The size of each circle corresponds to the importance you assigned to it in the first column of the four-way attention chart. If, for example, "Work" was 30 percent and "Home" was 40 percent, then the "Home" circle would be about one-third bigger than the "Work" circle. In this case, work is less important than home.

- **Think about relative location.** The second choice is each circle's *location in relation to the others*: do they overlap or are they separate? Where you place your four circles, how much they overlap represents your best estimate of how compatible or incompatible the domains are with each other. Complete *harmony* between any two domains— which exists when the aims in one domain, and your way of achieving them, fit perfectly with the other domain—would be represented by complete overlap of the two representative circles. Complete incompatibility, or *conflict*, between any two domains—when your actions and their results in one are antagonistic to the other—would be shown by representative circles that have no overlap at all.

Now you are ready to draw your circles. Take a piece of paper or go to www.totalleadership.org, and draw four circles, each representing one of the four domains: work, home, community, and self. Write the name of each domain in or around the corresponding circle.

Begin to write down your thoughts. One way to think about achieving greater authenticity is to imagine what you would have to do to have a life illustrated by four completely overlapping circles. Keep in mind that few people have completely overlapping circles; this is an image to aim for. What are your ideas for how you might pursue goals in such a way as to achieve greater overlap, or compatibility, and to reduce conflict among domains?

### Imagine the Perfect Center of a Tree

Complete overlap of all four domains is, of course, extraordinarily rare. It's hard to conceive of a real life in which the goals you seek and the way you act in all aspects of your life are in pure harmony. The best examples might be those of great religious leaders—the likes of Buddha, Christ, Mohammed, the Dalai Lama, and Moses. In the lives of these exemplars, the purposes pursued by the private person were essentially the same as those sought in the context of their work, family, and society.

But since you're human, not divine, don't worry if your four circles don't line up exactly. Indeed, if you drew your circles to look like the perfect center of a strong tree's trunk, with all four domains concentric around a common core, then please return this book immediately and contact me to arrange an interview! Consider that complete incompatibility between any two domains—circles that have no common area at all—is not uncommon. There is almost always some conflict, in the real world, between who you are in one part of your life and who you are in the other parts.

It's useful to identify areas of compatibility, as well as of discord, among life domains, for this helps you to see the harmony that already exists, and so gives you ideas for expanding it. You'll start to ask, "If I can do it here, why not there . . . and there?"

This picture serves as an instrument to help you think about the relationships among the different parts of your life. The center of a tree is an ideal to strive for, and the contrast between it and your current picture, the one you just drew, can lead you to new ideas for taking action to increase your authenticity. The closer you can get to entirely overlapping domains, in other words, the more likely you're being the person you want to be, wherever you are and in whatever role you're in at that moment.

### Learning from the Four Circles

We read what Victor thought about when he examined his responses to the four-way attention chart. Now let's look at how he drew his four circles, shown in figure 3-1.

This image painfully revealed to Victor that there was no overlap whatsoever between his work and family domains.

> Work is pretty much out there on its own. There is some overlap with my self domain, as I get a good feeling about my self from having a successful working life. But that's pretty much it. I find this rather distressing! And there is not much overlap between my self and family domains at the moment. I really must do something about this.

What Victor realized when analyzing the picture he drew of his four circles is that, among other things, the person he is at work—the goals and interests he pursues as an IT director at an investment bank—is entirely different from the father and husband he wants to be at home. In Victor's leadership vision, parts of which you read in chapter 2, he wrote about having his children engaged in his work and also about applying

FIGURE 3-1

**Victor's four circles**

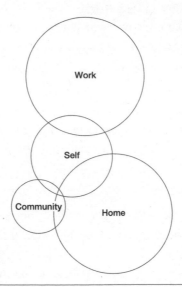

skills he developed teaching his children music to his managerial responsibilities at work. There was some overlap between work and home domains in that leadership vision, but there were none that he could see in
his current life circumstances. What Victor learned was discouraging to
him, but it was a wake-up call, a seed of transformation. Already, Victor
had clarified what's important to him. He began to create new insights
about possible four-way wins.

One goal of the Total Leadership process is to create change in order
to produce harmony among your four domains. You can learn, in other
words, from your four circles by asking what you would have to do to
have them overlapping. You might start by looking, for example, at your
work. Would you have to change your career entirely to bring it closer to
the person you are in your family? Or, instead, would you have to change

how you think about what you do at work as it relates to your family, your role in society, and your mind, body, and spirit? Another way to approach this issue is to ask about the purpose of your career: is it to earn money to keep you and your loved ones fed and sheltered, to enjoy the material things in life, or is there something about it that makes you feel proud about the impact you're having on the world through your work? And if so, how does this feeling affect how your friends and family see you? Further, what would you have to change to make this feeling grow and be more a part of your everyday experience of your work and career? Would you have to *act* differently, or would you have to *think* differently about what you're accomplishing through your work?

Now let's consider questions about your home and family. What changes would you have to make to bring this part of your life into harmony with the other parts? Let's say you're a student just about to graduate college, for example. Would you have to change the level of dependence you now have on your parents? If so, how might you do this in a way that would be good for them and for you? Or let's say you're living in an intimate relationship with someone who has different values from yours and doesn't support the role you're playing in society. Should you end the relationship? Less drastically, perhaps, is there a way to change how she sees this other part of your life so that she becomes more supportive of it?

Pondering such questions as you look at your four circles generates ideas for specific things you might do to achieve greater compatibility and less conflict.

Roxanne's drawing of her four circles (see figure 3-2) was quite different from Victor's.

Even though there is no overlap between Roxanne's self and work domains—in other words, her professional life just isn't in sync with what she wants for her self in promoting a healthy mind, body, and spirit—there is quite a lot of overlap otherwise. For instance, through her role as a mother and as a business professional, she feels she's making valuable

FIGURE 3-2

**Roxanne's four circles**

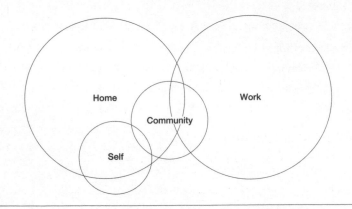

contributions to society in raising her children and in selling chemical products that improve health care.

In studying her four circles, Roxanne began to have some thoughts about things she could do to produce even greater overlap.

> I tend to work at home on the weekends, mainly because, I'm em-
> barrassed to admit, I've just not been creative enough to find some-
> thing more engaging to do with my family that's good for all of us. I
> guess I've been driven by the belief that all my investments in work
> will free up my time to do other things later—and it's always
> *later*—when something more important is planned for our family.
>     Maybe I can plan some things to do now with my family—like
> golf, tennis, swimming—that are also things I want to do for my-
> self. Or I can plan family activities that support what I'd like to
> be doing for our local community. Or I can become involved with

already existing work activities that support the community, such as the United Way.

Just as it was for Roxanne, the picture you draw of your four circles is another tool for stimulating your thinking about how *you* might create better harmony among your life domains. But we're not quite done with the four-way view of your life's domains.

## Domain Satisfaction:
## Your Four-Way Happiness Rating

Now assess whether or not you're satisfied with each domain, and with your life as a whole. In other words, are you happy with how things are going?

## DOMAIN SATISFACTION— THE FOUR-WAY HAPPINESS RATING

Indicate how satisfied you are presently with how things are going in each domain, and for your life as a whole, by writing a number from 1 to 10, where 1 = not at all satisfied and 10 = fully satisfied, in the appropriate column.

| Domain | Satisfaction |
|---|---|
| Work/Career/School | |
| Home/Family | |
| Community/Society | |
| Self: mind, body, spirit | |
| Life as a whole | |

## Just a Matter of Time?

So what is it about the relationship among the four domains that affects whether you feel satisfied? How you spend your time matters, of course. But, it turns out that, surprising as it might seem, managing your time is *not* the major factor. In a study described in *Work and Family— Allies or Enemies?* Jeff Greenhaus and I found that while the "time bind" so often cited in the literature on work/family conflict is no doubt very real, there is a more subtle and pervasive problem that reduces satisfaction in the different domains of life: psychological interference between them.[1] That's when your mind is pulled to somewhere other than where your body is. This happens to all of us. There may even be times when you've been reading this book and your eyes are on the page but your mind has drifted off. You aren't focused. Put differently, there are times when you might be physically present but psychologically absent—something people can usually tell because it affects your ability to connect with them.

If you reduce psychological interference, you increase your ability to focus on *what* matters *when* it matters, and you minimize the destructive impact conflicts can cause between, for instance, work and family. A main premise of this book is that it takes leadership skill to manage the boundaries between the different areas of your life—not just the physical boundaries of time and space, but the psychological boundaries of focus and attention—and to integrate them well for mutual gain.

Being real by demonstrating authenticity is a necessary first step. You must assess the relationship between what's important and where you devote your time. But you must also understand the implications of what your four circles mean to you. André, the married father of two young children and product manager for a global software developer, had this to say about what he learned from his analysis of the relationships among his four domains:

When I first thought about creating the four circles, I realized that I had been looking at my life domains as separate wedges of a pie rather than as circles that could overlap. In other words, I was viewing my life—and its different parts—as a zero-sum game where to give to one part, I had to take from somewhere else. And where did it get me? When I took actions to make things better in one domain, it always meant decreasing my satisfaction in another domain.

I believe this is why I find it so difficult to be fully engaged in the different domains. So often, I just feel as if I'm being pulled in different directions. When I try to prioritize things, I end up failing to meet expectations and do what people legitimately expect of me. That makes me dissatisfied.

Looking at the domains this way has helped me realize that I have to change my thought process and find new ways to integrate the different areas of my life. They do overlap, and they need to overlap. They're not separate pieces of the pie.

Is it possible to have your pie and eat it too? The evidence I've seen convinces me that it is—certainly more so than most people believe. Getting there means taking steps to ensure that the goals you're pursuing in each domain of your life are mutually enriching *and* consistent with your core values and aspirations. Does this mean you need to change how you spend your time? Probably, and it might also mean change in how you think about what you're doing with the time you're spending.

Clarifying what's important enhances your sense of authenticity, of being who you want to be. You can take control and create for yourself a life where you do not always have to trade success and satisfaction in one domain for success and satisfaction in another.

When you've clarified what's important to you, you become more of a leader who acts with authenticity, whose values and actions are aligned. When you lead with authenticity, it's easier to get support from the important people in your life. This book is not about striking a balance between work and the rest of life. It is about identifying your values—what's important to you—and making them come alive in your everyday actions at work, at home, in the community, and for your self.

Having done all this soul searching, looking within, you'll now look outward in the next steps on this journey.

## PAUSE AND REFLECT ON YOUR FOUR-WAY VIEW

Here are things to keep in mind as you synthesize what you've done in chapter 3 before moving on to chapter 4. Read through your responses to the exercises in this chapter. Consider the following questions. Write about them and then, if possible, talk about them with your coach.

1. What are the main ideas you take away from what you've just read?

2. What is the biggest disconnect in the relationship among your four domains?

3. What changes might you make to bring the four domains of your life into greater harmony?

4. How would such changes affect your happiness ratings?

# PART II

# BE WHOLE
## Act with Integrity

## CHAPTER 4

# Respect the Whole Person

T O BE WHOLE is to live a life in which the parts are integrated in a way that makes sense and has coherence. Integrity, while usually referring to sincerity and honor, refers here to the strength inherent in a well-designed structure or system, as in the statement "Frank Lloyd Wright's Fallingwater has great integrity." The whole fits together elegantly. Effective leaders tap into that power by recognizing and respecting all aspects of life, maintaining the boundaries that enable productive effort in each domain while taking advantage of resources from one by applying it in others. To get better at doing so, you'll start by identifying the most important people in each part of your life, describing what you expect from each other, and seeing how these expectations form an interacting system of relationships that you can influence to become more consistent with what you care about most.

Victor did this. Between his wife, his two children, and his many colleagues at the New York investment bank where he directs information technology, Victor answers to a host of different people. Asked to reflect on what he needs to be successful in the most critical relationships in his life, he said:

> Each of the people in my immediate family wants the same things from me: to be loving, present, and supportive. And I want to feel rested and energized, and to feel good about how I spend my time.
>
> At work, people expect me to deliver and to add real value. But people at work also want to feel positive about our interactions. In fact, feeling good about interacting with me seems to be a common theme with people in different areas of my life.
>
> I'm starting to see more clearly that this is closely related to how I want to feel about myself. Being positive in my interactions is directly connected to whether I feel relaxed and generally good about myself. If I feel rested and energized, won't I deliver better results for my business? Won't I be better able to really pay attention at home? This is something to work on.

In looking to the most important people in his life, Victor began to discern patterns and themes, as well as areas of both compatibility and conflict. In this second part of the Total Leadership experience, you view things from the outside, taking stock of your relationships with what I call your "key stakeholders," the people who really matter to you. We'll expand and deepen the notion of "performance expectations" to see how it applies to *all* of your key stakeholders, not just to your boss at work. You'll ask not just what they expect from you and what you expect of them, but also how well these expectations are being met today. Finally, you'll take a fresh look at the media through which you actually stay connected with them.

Building on the foundation you established in the previous chapters, once you complete these assessments about your key stakeholders you'll be in a much better position to decide what you can do to better align your interests with theirs and how you can enrich your connections with them for mutual benefit. The goal is to strengthen these relationships and to transform how you feel about the people around you. For many past participants, this has meant going from feeling resentment over what others were demanding and being pulled in too many different directions, to feeling supported by close associates and so better able to respond confidently to life's challenges.

Assessing what your key stakeholders expect from you, what you need from them, and how you stay in touch with them takes time, but it's an important step in the Total Leadership process. If you understand the stuff of what and who matters most to you, you will have more meaningful opportunities to integrate the pieces of your life in new ways.

## Identifying Key Stakeholders

Key stakeholders are the people who have a *stake* in your future. They exist at work, at home, and in your community. And in the fourth domain—that is, your mind, body, and spirit—you are the key stakeholder, the most complicated stakeholder of all!

A stakeholder could be your boss or your child. It could be your spouse, roommate, or partner. It could be another student in your class or a peer in your department at work. Your stakeholders could also be the leaders of your religious group, the members of your sports club, or friends and neighbors. You might also think of the greater society and the environment as stakeholders in your life. In short, your stakeholders can be anyone and can be anywhere—in any aspect of your world that you deem important.

To identify your key stakeholders is to make choices about who is most important. Consider who in each domain has the most impact on your life. Take into account how much you interact with this person or group. How does this relationship bear on what you believe in and what you're trying to accomplish?

There's no formula for who you identify as your key stakeholders. It's up to you, and only you, to figure out who they are. Be prepared to change your list. When you articulate the expectations you have of people and the expectations you think they have of you, it's not uncommon to realize that people you thought *are* or *should be* key stakeholders really are not. Just doing this part of the analysis helps define the centrality of the roles people play in your life. It can be liberating, for example, to

## WHO MATTERS MOST?

In this exercise you list the names of your four or five key stakeholders in each domain—in your work or career, in your home or family, and in the community or society.

Consider these questions to identify your key stakeholders:

- Who are the most important people, groups, or other entities (e.g., animals, the environment) to you in each of these domains?

- With whom in each domain do you have the most frequent contact?

- Who are the people with the greatest amount of influence on your life and the people on whose lives you exert a great deal of influence?

Once you've thought this through, make a list of the names of these people or groups, one for each of the three domains other than the self domain, which we'll get to shortly. It's a good idea to write a sentence or two about why you chose each of them.

decide that certain people are no longer key stakeholders. It doesn't mean you don't care about them. It just means that your relationship now is different than it might once have been. College students, for example, often realize that their relationships with their parents are entering a new phase. Similarly, a colleague from a former career may become more of a social friend than a work friend.

### Victor's Stakeholders

When Victor thought about his key stakeholders at work, he listed the vice president to whom he reports, one of his peers at his organizational level, the team of people who report to him, and the other students in his executive MBA program. In his home domain he identified his wife, his son and daughter, and his parents. Finally, for his community, he listed his friends, his neighborhood community center, and a volunteer mentoring program in which he was involved. These were the people in what you might call Victor's inner circle—the people he saw, at least at that time, as being most important to him.

Simply listing those in your inner circle is just the start. Later in the Total Leadership process, you will design experiments to produce four-way wins, in which people in all your domains benefit from changes you make. To do this effectively, you must know what a "win" really looks like from the point of view of those who matter to you. It's necessary, then, to begin by thinking about the critical people in various domains of your life and to explore what you can do, now and in the future, to help them achieve whatever it is *they* care about.

## What Do Your Key Stakeholders Expect of You?

Building meaningful connections with people on whose support you depend is a sine qua non of leadership. It's difficult, if not impossible, to inspire others to get important things done unless they believe in you and what you're trying to achieve. Think of the person you identified as a hero in chapter 2. I'll bet that she was seen by people around her as trustworthy and that her credibility was based, at least in part, on her capacity to see things from others' perspectives. Doing so gives you the power to help them see the benefits of what you are trying to achieve and how and why they should support you.

Once you've identified your stakeholders, the next step is to consider what you think they expect from you. Imagine how they view their relationship with you. What do they really need from you? What do you think good performance from you looks like from their perspective?

## EXPECTATIONS STAKEHOLDERS HAVE OF YOU

Begin to complete the stakeholder expectations chart below by first writing the name of each stakeholder in the appropriate box.

Then, put yourself in the mind of each of your stakeholders, one at a time. Imagine how each would respond to this question: what are the main things you want or need from me? Describe the behaviors he or she expects, being as specific as you can. Write your response in each box.

In the last column are different aspects of the self domain. Write in each box what you expect of yourself with respect to spirituality, relaxation, and physical and emotional health. Again, be as specific as possible.

Finally, in the upper right-hand corner of each stakeholder box, identify the degree to which you feel you are meeting the performance expectations you described, using a scale of 1 to 10. A 10 indicates that you believe you are meeting expectations fully, all of the time. A 5 indicates that you believe you are meeting expectations some of the time. A 1 indicates that you believe you are never meeting these expectations.

# Stakeholder Expectations Chart: 1

| Work | Home | Community | Self | |
|---|---|---|---|---|
| | | | Spirituality | |
| | | | Relaxation | |
| | | | Physical health | |
| | | | Emotional health | |

With the first part of your stakeholder expectations chart complete, you now have an opportunity to think about several important questions that you probably haven't considered before. Take some time now to do so and write short notes in response to these questions:

- What are the main things my stakeholders really want from me, including, but also beyond, my time and attention?
- Are there ways in which the expectations one stakeholder in one domain has of me are compatible with those of a stakeholder in a different domain? Do they mesh in some way?
- Where do they conflict?
- Do these expectations fit with my values and what I want to achieve in the future?
- What might I do differently as a result of my answers to these questions?

### *What Victor Thinks His Stakeholders Expect of Him*

Victor identified the main things each stakeholder or cluster of stakeholders expected of him, and thought about what he wrote:

The expectations are more compatible with each other than I thought they'd be. At home, there's a huge overlap with respect to what my family members expect from me ("be present," "be around," "stay in touch"). The same goes for my work stakeholders. And being positive in my family and my work interactions is compatible with my own desire to feel relaxed, centered, and generally good about myself.

Yet there are different pulls, which seem to be resolved only by compromise. It's difficult to be at home and focused on my wife and kids while trying to deliver at work and also trying to finish a paper for school. It's difficult to do all this and also take time out for myself.

Of course, time matters, and, alas, it's limited. But think about how, from what you know about Victor, he might try some new way of spending his time that might produce a four-way win. What could he do to reduce the trade-offs and improve results all the way around? When you read your stakeholder expectations chart you might, like Victor, see lack of time as the big stumbling block in realizing the full potential of your most important relationships. But there's more to the picture than first meets the eye, as we'll see. As you take the next steps in this book, you'll expand your awareness of how and why you can use your time better.

## What Do You Expect of Them?

Let's now flip the tables. Once you've articulated what you think your stakeholders expect of you—and how well you're doing in meeting those expectations—it's useful to describe the support you need from them to achieve your goals and to integrate the four domains of your life.

---

### EXPECTATIONS YOU HAVE OF STAKEHOLDERS

First, write the names of your key stakeholders on this second version of your stakeholder expectations chart.

Then, write what you see as the main things you want or need from each of them. Describe the behaviors you expect, being as specific as you can. Write your response in each box.

As before, in the upper right-hand corner of each stakeholder box, identify the degree to which you feel each stakeholder is meeting the performance expectations you described, using a scale of 1 to 10. A 10 indicates that you believe this stakeholder is meeting expectations fully, all of the time. A 5 indicates that you believe this stakeholder is meeting expectations some of the time. A 1 indicates that you believe this stakeholder is never meeting these expectations.

# Stakeholder Expectations Chart: 2

| Work | Home | Community |
|------|------|-----------|
| | | |
| | | |
| | | |
| | | |

With the second part of your stakeholder expectations chart complete, take a few more minutes to write short notes in response to these questions:

- Overall, what are the main things you really want and need from your key stakeholders?

- How compatible are your expectations for them with what they expect of you?

- How do your expectations for them fit with what you wrote earlier in this book about what is really important to you?

### What Victor Expects of His Stakeholders

Victor filled in his chart of the performance expectations he had for the key stakeholders he identified in his previous chart, along with his assessment of how well they were doing in meeting these expectations (on the same scale of 1 to 10). Victor then answered questions about this chart, looking for patterns.

A common thread runs through the main things I really want and need from my key stakeholders. I work pretty hard in my business, and I want to be rewarded and appreciated for my results. Or if they aren't valued, I want some direction as to how I can address any issues. The same applies to my family life. I feel that I actually do a fair amount of the household chores, child care, and so on. I need to be appreciated for that.

These expectations are largely compatible with what my stakeholders expect of me. It seems to be a fair trade to deliver the expected results at work and expect to be rewarded for them. Similarly,

I expect my team members to deliver, and in return they need to feel respected; they need to feel that their careers are growing. At home, my wife's expectation that I share the load in raising the kids and doing household chores doesn't fit with my need for her support while I work out the final months of my executive MBA program and also try to keep my working life progressing.

I'm pleased to find that my expectations fit fairly well with my future aspirations. Respect is one of my core values, and it's a common theme with my stakeholders. Being supportive is a theme that runs through expectations in both directions. I didn't mention that in my initial draft of my leadership vision, but I realize now how important this is at work, at home, and in the community.

Victor is starting to see in new ways how the different domains are all part of one system in which the elements affect each other. Likewise, the exercises you've just done are designed to help you grasp the whole of your four domains, with an appreciation for the interdependent connections among those domains.

## Seeing Your Life as a System

The emphasis on the mutually reinforcing influences of the different parts gets to one of the most profound changes that happen in the Total Leadership process. That is, you get smarter about what it means to be whole, to fit the pieces of the puzzle that is your life into a coherent, integral system.

You start by observing patterns. What do you see when you review your charts? Do you see how the parts really do affect each other? You will start to see more clearly where the boundaries are between the parts and how important it is to manage them.

A boundary is anything marking a limit; here we use the term to denote the mark between different domains of life. Boundaries between domains vary in how *permeable* they are (whether they are open or closed to blending) and in how *flexible* they are (whether or not they are easily changed). It is possible to play with boundaries by combining or, on the other hand, segmenting different domains. Victor saw this possibility:

> I'm beginning to see how important it might be to address the boundaries between the different areas of my life. I need to create stronger boundaries between domains that will allow me to focus on what matters most at any given time, but also ensure that my boundaries don't keep me from satisfying stakeholder interests that cross domains.

Victor is starting to engage in the creative process of transformation: he realizes how he might practice being both psychologically and physically present and thus more effective in a given role, which would, in turn, make him feel better about his performance, feel more satisfied, and feel a positive impact across the domains of his life.

Jenna, too, saw for the first time how stakeholder performance expectations affect each other when she thought about what she saw in her charts:

> Identifying what I think my stakeholders expect of me was a revelation. It made me realize that what my family really needs from me is acceptance. For instance, my father and sister are so different from me, and I often find it difficult just to accept them for who they are. So, I try to compensate by being especially attentive toward them in other ways. Clearly, they're after something else, and I have to figure out how to meet their legitimate expectations.
>
> At work, I'd never really thought—at least in any systematic way—about how the people I manage rely on me not just for the day-to-day supervision and motivation, but also as an enabler of their success. I was really excited to realize that it is true that we all feed

off of each other's successes, which means their expectation that I succeed is not just an expectation, but something they need.

Like Victor's, Jenna's realizations are steps toward being more whole. You're demonstrating integrity when you respect your key stakeholders and seek to unify dissimilar expectations (yours and theirs) through creative action that flows from your values. You can't make this happen unless you know what you and your stakeholders expect of each other.

Your journey toward becoming the leader you want to be requires taking time to think through your perceptions of stakeholder expectations. You can identify new opportunities to improve performance by, for example, combining tasks to meet multiple stakeholder expectations (a direct win for all four domains). Or for another example, you might manage boundaries more effectively, protecting time for action in a given domain and explaining to people who matter why this time is needed and— *this is most important*—how such boundaries serve them *and* you well (a direct win for one or two domains and an indirect win for the others).

## SEE YOUR LIFE AS A SYSTEM
## YOU CAN CHANGE

In this exercise, draw from your stakeholder expectations charts to stimulate ideas about what you might do to produce four-way wins. Write brief responses to the following questions:

- In which domain are you doing best in meeting expectations? Where are you doing worst?
- Is the solution to be found with you or them?
- Which relationships would be easiest to change? Why?
- Which would be hardest? Why?

> • How can you improve satisfaction and performance in one
>   domain by improving performance in other domains? For
>   example, how might you improve your work performance by
>   improving performance in your community or at home?

Your answers to these questions help you to see that your stake-holder relationships are all part of a whole—*your life*—and help you no-tice connections between the parts. What happens in one domain, or even with a single stakeholder, affects the others. And as a leader, you can influence whether this mutual impact is beneficial or not. You can take action to close what I call "stakeholder performance gaps."

To find your gaps, compare the performance ratings for your stake-holders on the two charts. Any number short of 10, in either direction, indicates a gap. The largest possible gap for any stakeholder, of course, would be where you scored a 1 for both you and your stakeholder.

Jenna offers a good example of the value of taking this kind of snap-shot of your life.

I consider myself a fabulous mother, partner to Cheryl, sister, daughter, and friend—but I'm doing worst in the home domain! Absolutely not the results I anticipated! I actually expected com-munity to be worst, followed by work. But I never considered these things so systematically, and now I realize that any solution that's going to improve my meeting of expectations, and vice versa, has to be found in both my stakeholders and me. It must involve a com-bination of striving to meet each other's expectations better and working together to modify each other's expectations and bring them into alignment.

This was a powerful insight for Jenna. It later motivated her experiments. But the most important question in exploring the implications of the gaps you see in your performance scores is the last one in previous exercise: How can you improve performance in one domain by closing a stakeholder performance gap in another domain? For example, how by being a better father do I become a better manager? How would improvement in the quality of my relationships with my friends make things better for my family and for my business? How would better physical health improve my productivity at work? Discovering answers to these kinds of questions is, in essence, an inquiry into how to produce greater integrity in your life.

## Finding Four-Way Wins

Most people think in terms of zero-sum "balance" solutions to the dilemma of how to integrate the various roles they play. I'm encouraging you to think differently, which can take a bit of imagination. Don't hold back. Open your mind to all the possible ways by which your goals, interests, and values in one domain benefit those in others.

The idea of four-way wins is a basic assumption for the Total Leadership method: there are opportunities for creating mutual gain among diverse stakeholders across different life domains. Not only can you create harmony among domains, but you can improve performance in them by transferring assets—skills, values, connections—from one domain to another. You can produce "positive spillover": for example, when you're feeling good about how you're performing as a parent, you can feel good and more focused in other parts of your life. Many Total Leadership participants report that improving performance at home, in the community, and in themselves results indirectly—by way of positive spillover—in their being more productive with their work.

Some Total Leadership participants, at least at the beginning, tend to focus on changes they want to make at work and ignore other domains.

Sometimes I have to prod them to adopt a broader, multiple-domain perspective. If you're intent on discovering four-way wins, then it can't all be about work; it's essential that you continually look for opportunities for realizing benefits in all four domains. If it's simply looking for performance gains within one or another domain, then it doesn't fit with the goals of Total Leadership.

Here is more of what Victor wrote in response to the questions in the last exercise:

> Clearly, I'm doing my best meeting expectations in the work domain; I'm worst in my self domain. And I'm not meeting expectations very well at home, which is the most important area to me. I guess it would be easiest to change things at home, since it's far easier to communicate about these kinds of expectations there than at work. The culture, the accepted modus operandi of interactions at work, gets in the way. Plus, my boss and I have simply never communicated on this level before. Our interactions have been about the job and little else. That's going to have to change.
>
> Looking at these charts, my gut reaction was first to focus on fixing things at home, since it's the area bothering me the most. But I've thought about it some more. Wouldn't that be focusing on the symptom and not the cure? I probably have to focus on home and on self at the same time—and I know I need to be thinking about how this will affect work and community, even if it's indirect. The key here is going to be doing this without introducing yet more competing demands on my limited time. I need to identify things that aren't onerous and that somehow make things better in all the different parts of my life.

Victor is drawing practical lessons from his assessments and thinking about how to apply those lessons to the design of his experiments. He has absorbed what is one of the most critical ideas in the Total Leadership approach. The point of this whole process is to *reduce* stress and pressure and to *increase* performance. The big idea is that if you look at your life as a whole, and if you pursue experiments in how you think and act—while getting others to see how it's in their best interests to support you—you will succeed in producing better results with fewer trade-offs. Things will get better and you'll feel more like the navigator of your life because you'll have learned how to be one in a way that works for you.

## Patterns of Stakeholder Relationships

It is helpful to differentiate between impulsive reactions and more thoughtful approaches to patterns you might see in your relationships.

First, there is what I call the "explosive" pattern, the situation in which expectations are hardly being met in either direction. No one's happy. What would a leader do to keep such a relationship working, to salvage and improve it? Clarify mutual expectations, reframe them, and innovate in how things get done. Indeed, that is what's to come in later chapters. All too often, though, people react impulsively to an explosive situation and run away from it, even when they know it would be better if they tried to make it work.

Then there is the "angry" pattern, in which you feel as if you're doing well for others, but that they are letting you down. What's the impulsive response to this scenario? Some turn their resentment inward and feel bad about themselves, even becoming depressed. Others strike out verbally. Some do both. A more productive response would be to clarify your own expectations with your stakeholders, explain the consequences for you and them of expectations being unmet, and—if indeed they *are* acceptable—accept limitations consciously.

Many people find that they put too much pressure on themselves because they inaccurately inflate the expectations others have of them. In the "pressure/guilt" pattern, it's as if the tables are turned from the angry type: everyone's doing right by you, but you're letting everyone down. Doing more of the same but trying harder, an impulsive response, often leads only to increased stress and strain. I've found that many

Total Leadership participants are trapped in this psychological pressure cooker. Asserting leadership here again means clarifying expectations, which can be very liberating. From there, negotiation and innovation are possible. Often, participants discover that the expectations others have of them are actually lower than what they had imagined, leading to lower stress and smart changes in the distribution of time and energy.

The opposite of explosive I call "expansive." This is when both parties are meeting expectations fully. If you see this, you've achieved a kind of perfection. Of course, it's next to impossible to imagine anyone honestly having a life that might be illustrated by this pattern in all stakeholder relationships; I've seen a thousand stakeholder expectations charts, but never a perfectly expansive one. If you had one, though, what would you do? Learn how you got there and continue to build on it, deepening your knowledge about how to cultivate productive relationships throughout all domains of your life.

## Media for Connecting with Key Stakeholders

Being whole requires that you stay connected with the people who matter to you. As someone living in the twenty-first century, your choice of the means by which you do this is not always obvious. It pays to give some thought to how you apply the incredibly powerful communication devices now available.

Digital technology has added both relief and stress to our lives. New tools promise to liberate us from the constraints of time and place, but they come with a host of new problems. They can make it easier to move rapidly from one domain to another and so make it easier to manage boundaries and give rapid access to the people who need you. And you can broadcast with them, making communication extremely efficient. Yet most people find themselves trapped by the demands imposed by the enormous amount of information surrounding them every hour of every day, failing to realize the potential benefits.

Let's do a thought experiment: if I told you right now that you had to give up all your digital devices for the next three days, how would you feel? Relieved? Terrified? We've become enormously dependent on these tools, and yet we've not spent nearly enough time thinking about how best to use them so that we gain the benefits while keeping them from reducing the quality of our lives.

Instead, people complain that using new technologies reduces social interaction and sense of community, while others rant about being expected to be available for work 24/7 with zero response time to urgent messages. While the promise of new media is freedom, choice, and control, the reality for most is crippling overload. On the employer side, many bosses wonder whether people really work when they are connecting virtually. They also worry about how to foster team spirit when the "team" is invisible. Finally, when performance is measured the old-fashioned way (by time spent in an office) and not on the basis of results (no matter where and when they are produced), digital communications can seem to undermine productivity.

We're just getting wise to the psychological and social technologies required to take full advantage of the tools the digital revolution has wrought. But what if you could use the media available to you to build trust and gain greater flexibility? And what if you could do this without being enslaved and constantly bombarded by your "CrackBerry," your cell phone, and your laptop? You'd be more whole, better able to integrate the diverse pieces of the social puzzle in your life.

You can learn to use new media to shift time and place in ways that work for all your stakeholders, including yourself. But the intelligent use of the various media we now have isn't just a matter of doing more digital. For some it's a matter of more consciously allocating your use of in-person contact, making face-to-face (F2F) communication a priority for those stakeholders with whom it's needed, while using digital less. It all depends on what's going to work best for you and for them.

Studying your forms of interaction will help you generate ideas for how you might capitalize on the benefits of each communication mode (e.g., face-to-face is best when trust is on the line) while minimizing the liabilities (e.g., face-to-face requires you to be in a certain place at a certain time). This might mean shifting to more in-person time with certain stakeholders (such as your children or clients) and less with others (such as with your boss or the people who report to you) while leveraging the flexibility of virtual media as a means of staying connected with others. Use the following exercise to stimulate creative thinking about exploiting various forms of communication.

## FORMS OF COMMUNICATION

Think about the media you use to communicate with your stakeholders. For each stakeholder, estimate the percentage of your interaction time that is conducted through each of three forms of communication: face-to-face, virtual synchronous (shifting place but not time, such as phone, instant messaging, and videoconferencing), and virtual asynchronous (shifting both time and place, such as voice mail and e-mail) communication. For example, you might spend 50 percent in F2F with your boss, 20 percent on the phone, and 30 percent by e-mail and voice mail. Find a convenient place to record the percentages for each of your stakeholders.

After you do so, look for patterns. Consider how using different forms of communication affects your capacity to achieve your goals in each domain and to align them. What opportunities are there for you to use different forms of communication more effectively? Are there stakeholders with whom you should be devoting more time F2F and others less? With whom would it be better to use virtual more regularly?

The real value in this analysis is to become more aware of media preferences (yours and theirs) and to learn more about how you can be more effective in meeting expectations by using a given medium. Look for opportunities to explain why you have a preference for one medium over another for certain kinds of communications. For example, if you prefer e-mail and can justify it as the option of choice rather than telephone to a friend, your father, or a coworker, that conversation about your preferences will probably make the entire process of communicating go smoother. The technology choice should be based on a mutual understanding about why, how, and when you're going to communicate.

Stay mindful of the preferences others have. In your stakeholder dialogues, you'll have the chance to talk about when, where, and how you use different media to stay connected, including when you're available and when you're not. You might, for instance, discuss what it would be like to shut off the digital information stream for a specific period—even for just an hour or two—to focus your attention entirely on one thing.

There are many ways of experimenting with your use of various media with the goal of producing four-way wins. Analyzing your use of technology sets the stage for smart experiments in its use, which we take up in the next part of the book. But new media are no panacea for misaligned domains, failure to meet stakeholder expectations, or failure to get what you need from your stakeholders.

In the next chapter, I'll show you how to conduct fruitful conversations—via whatever medium makes the most sense—with the key stakeholders in your life, all in a concentrated period of time, about what you've been writing and thinking about in this and previous chapters. The preparation you've just completed—identifying the most important people, describing what you expect of each other and how well these expectations are being met, seeing how the different parts affect each other, and assessing how you use communication tools to stay connected with them—will serve you well as you take the next steps toward building greater integrity in your life.

Before moving on, pause and reflect on the main ideas you've gleaned from your analysis of stakeholder expectations, and what you've learned about what it means for you to be whole.

## CHAPTER 5

# Talk to Your Stakeholders

O NCE VICTOR HAD CONSIDERED and reconsidered his relationships with those in his inner circle, he was prepared to start bringing these people closer to him. He was ready to begin *stakeholder dialogues*: conversations that delve into those relationships and, by revealing how they affect each other, create new opportunities for improving them all. To be a better leader and have a richer life, you have to continually practice the art of meaningful conversation with those you hope to inspire. You can never be too good at it.

Stakeholder dialogues have two main goals: to *verify* existing expectations and to, if it makes sense, *change* existing expectations—to explore how they might be met in new ways. Stakeholder dialogues provide an opportunity to build trust and enhance support from your inner circle. The one that proved most important for Victor at work, not surprisingly, was with his boss.

I didn't really anticipate that these dialogues would go well. I was afraid that people would be dismissive of what I was asking of them, and that they wouldn't engage in any meaningful way. But I was surprised, especially by the openness with which people approached our conversations, and how by just initiating these conversations, I was suddenly discussing things I never get to with many people. And it was easy to do!

The conversation I was dreading most was with my boss. He and I have little more than a mechanical "get the work done" sort of relationship, and I thought a dialogue with him would be a disaster. But even this one went much better than I anticipated. Once I laid out what I wanted and explained that I was doing this to up my performance across the board, we talked at an entirely new level. This may have been because he was pleased that I was asking him to confirm what I think he needs most from me. I'm not saying we're close now, but it's a start—a step in the direction I want to go.

Stakeholder dialogues will propel you to the next step, designing experiments that will benefit not just you but all the important people in your life. This is, after all, *the* leadership challenge: to choose a meaningful direction, based on knowing yourself and your people, and then to gain commitment to its vigorous pursuit.

## What You Gain from Stakeholder Dialogues

The steps of the Total Leadership program build one upon another. The work you did in the first few chapters established the foundation: you contemplated your core values, imagined the leader you want to become, assessed how satisfied you are, looked at how well you are performing in the different areas of your life, and determined how well you are collaborating with the people most important to you.

Now, in your stakeholder dialogues, you confirm and, in some cases, correct your perceptions about performance expectations. You take both a broad and a deep look at your primary relationships to see more vividly the web of connections in which you're embedded. These conversations help you to discern how different parts of your life affect each other. You discover shared interests with and among your stakeholders and unearth new ways of pursuing them. You can begin to discuss, either explicitly or implicitly, ideas for things you might try to change, to better serve your stakeholders' interests as well as your own.

Again, you don't *have* to reveal anything to others that you'd rather keep private. Throughout this whole process, you have full control over what you choose to let others know. But as you read earlier, telling your story—about your past and your future—is part of a leader's toolkit, so it's good to practice. Sharing your leadership vision helps your stakeholders join you wholeheartedly as you walk on down that road. In the stakeholder dialogues, you have a chance to tell your story to people who are the most interested in hearing it.

These dialogues, undertaken separately but within a concentrated period of time with each one of your key stakeholders, also give you feedback from people at work, at home, and in your community. In this sense they are similar to professional "360-degree feedback", that is, they solicit input from colleagues in the full circle surrounding you rather than just the standard practice of a performance review from your boss. But with stakeholder dialogues, you control the data collection, it doesn't bear on your compensation, and it's about *all* your life roles. Think of it as "life 360-degree feedback."

Stakeholder dialogues offer a fresh assessment of just how critical your closest relationships are to your success. To pursue your goals and live according to the values you hold dear, you will find it useful to know more about what others really want from you and to have a genuine discussion about what you need from them.

These differ from other conversations you might have in that they are built around work you've done so far. They are set up to help you see things from your stakeholders' points of view—from the outside in—an essential leadership skill. Your dialogues represent a turning point. They can transform your perspective and have a major impact on what's next. To gain all this requires some preparation and a plan.

## Chart Your Course

The assessments you completed in chapter 4 were based on your view of what your stakeholders expect. Of course, your perceptions might not be accurate. So, in preparing for your stakeholder dialogues, be open to surprise. Keep in mind that the primary purpose of these conversations is to confirm or correct your current understanding of stakeholder expectations. This gives you a more realistic, complete picture of what all your intimates want from you, and it helps you to see them as one whole system. This is a lot to accomplish. Anything more—like negotiating new expectations or discussing how to meet expectations better— is a bonus.

Every dialogue will be different, so you'll benefit from a plan for how to approach each one. Before you start, then, it's useful to think about how you want things to go. What issues do you want to focus on? Are there any topics you should avoid? What are you mainly looking to learn? Would it be best to have a formal or an informal discussion? In what order would it be best to address particular topics? How will you know when you've achieved your goals for each dialogue?

If you're like most past participants, you'll find that people will feel honored to be selected as one of your key stakeholders (that is, if you let them know that they are), and they will be pleased to talk with you about your mutual future. Make your stakeholders as comfortable as possible so that they feel good about this exchange. Give some thought to the right setting, medium, and time.

While face-to-face communication is usually best, it's not always preferable or possible. Is face-to-face communication necessary? If you take advantage of the flexibility that virtual communication provides will you still come away with the other person feeling closer? Consider the relative advantages and disadvantages of different media, and use this as a chance to build your capacity for making smart choices about how to use them.

While the Total Leadership experience starts out as your project, your stakeholders are essential to your success. Ultimately, they've got to feel that this process is theirs and that they support what you're trying to accomplish. The main point to remember in setting the stage for successful dialogues is to make them natural and easy for others, so that they end up feeling better about you than they did before.

Covering personal topics might make it difficult to jump right in, so allow ample time for the dialogues. Choose a location that makes you both relaxed. With people who report to you, for example, if you conduct dialogues in your office, they might be reminded too much of their subordinate position and therefore might be reluctant to tell you what they expect from you and where you might be falling short. A neutral location is generally best. And pick a place with minimum distractions. Try to set a time at which you anticipate no interruptions or as few as possible.

Before starting each dialogue, review what you wrote in chapter 4 and consider how you think your stakeholder feels about you and your performance in the relationship. It will help for you to think through your expectations of them, too. You'll refresh your understanding of your abiding interest in this person (or the group he or she represents) and have in mind opportunities for improvement *before* you talk. This will make it easier to negotiate new expectations, should you decide to go there in your dialogues.

It's a good idea to weave in some of the things you wrote about previously, especially your leadership vision, the story of your future. Think ahead about discussing your vision in such a way as to inspire them to see that what you're trying to achieve is good for them and for you. How, in other words, is each one of your stakeholders part of a collective future with you?

A bit of preparation goes a long way toward increasing the chances that these conversations will yield the results you want, making you a better leader. This next exercise helps you prepare for achieving the main purpose of these dialogues: verifying and confirming performance expectations. Following the guidelines here usually results in both parties feeling better about their relationship, more closely connected, and more supportive of each other's aims.

## REFINE YOUR APPROACH

Here are some suggestions for how to get at the main content of the exchange. Choose language that feels comfortable to you:

- Discuss your perception of what you believe they need from you, using "I statements" ("I think that you expect me to . . ."), and ask whether your perception is correct. If it's not, ask for clarification.

- Ask for details and examples of what they need from you and want for you.

- Flip it around and discuss your expectations of them, then ask for reactions and questions.

It's easy to fall into the trap of defending your past actions. Try not to let emotion get in the way of your understanding. Avoid blaming them for problems that may exist in your relationship. Be sensitive to their feelings by acknowledging them. And keep the main goal in mind: to verify and, if need be, correct your perceptions of mutual performance expectations.

In this process of discovery, you're doing what a scientist does: exploring. The more you can proceed with an inquiring mind, the better you'll grasp the expectations that surround you and, in turn, the more intelligent and successful will be the experiments you design in the next chapter.

Now, take some time to write your initial thoughts about:

1. How to set up each dialogue—including the timing, setting, and medium.

2. What to bring from previous chapters.

3. What you'll do to verify performance expectations with each stakeholder.

Each relationship is different, and each person will react uniquely to the opportunity for conversation. Consider how you'll confirm your perceptions about what each stakeholder expects of you, and vice versa, and then how you can find out more about these expectations so that you have a good grasp of what they really mean to both of you.

## Working Through Your Fears

Another important aspect of preparing for your dialogues is to anticipate your own anxiety. Indeed, if you don't have some trepidation, then something's amiss; you're probably not thinking about it enough! It's normal to be wondering what will happen if you hear something you really don't want to hear. The preparation you're doing now will reduce the chances that any fears you have will be realized, and increase the likelihood of taking away useful insights from these conversations.

André learned this in preparing for his conversations with his wife, Marta.

In writing about my stakeholders' expectations, I was digging into my own weaknesses and innermost fears, and so I had reservations about sharing all this with Marta. She expects me to be strong, I thought, and I didn't want to have an adverse influence on her perception of me. Also, since she's under so much stress caring for our two young children, I didn't want to come across as too critical of her. But I felt that I needed to communicate some of my own expectations of her that I felt she wasn't fully meeting.

I was sure there would be some resistance and even resentment, but the conversation went surprisingly well. First, Marta validated a lot of my own perceptions, and this quickly diffused the tension I was feeling. She also told me that the financial expectations I had for myself about supporting our family were too extreme. She said that my personal view of what success meant financially was way in excess of what she thought we needed. She just wants to be comfortable, and has no need for, and little interest in, the level of financial security I had in mind for us.

And it was a great relief when she acknowledged areas where she could do better. They were the same things I was thinking of. Overall, my wife and I reaffirmed our love and commitment to each other. I'm sure it wasn't news to either of us that we still loved each other, but there was something really special about having this kind of conversation, this way.

André's dialogue wasn't just another rehash of old material, but a focused exchange about what really matters to both of them. It was an opportunity to assess expectations from both directions, and it surfaced ways that he and Marta could increase satisfaction at home.

Surprises are common: it usually turns out that most people expect less of you than you think they expect, and, conversely, they are more

willing to support you than you think they are. You're bound to be pleas-
antly surprised, that is. Not in every case, of course, but that's the most
likely result.

One of the most common sources of anxiety is anticipating a dialogue with your "dreaded stakeholder"—a term invented by one of my
students. Everyone seems to have at least one of these on their roster.
Who is the dreaded stakeholder, and what is so fearsome about this person? For any number of reasons, this is the one you desperately don't
want to talk to about your future and about how things are going now.
You might fear that he's going to take advantage of any vulnerability you
show by telling him about your hopes and dreams. Perhaps you worry
you'll hear that what you're planning for your life is foolishly unattain-
able—or downright silly. Usually the dreaded stakeholder is someone to
whom you've given a kind of power over you, someone you believe con-
trols some aspect of your life and is keeping you, or will keep you, from
doing something you want to do.

What I've found is that most dialogues with dreaded stakeholders
turn out better than anticipated, precisely because you prepare in advance, you adopt a spirit of inquiry (with a goal of knowledge rather
than victory), and you focus on a common future in which you both have
a stake. Taking this approach shows respect and opens the way toward
mutual support.

Lim was taken aback by the dialogue with his dreaded stakeholder:

By about 10 million light-years, the biggest surprise in my work domain was the dialogue with Sam, my boss. Not only was he open to
talking, but he seemed genuinely touched that I valued our relationship enough to have the dialogue in the first place. Honestly,
I'd come close to writing off this relationship altogether.

Our dialogue produced a breakthrough insight. He and I have
spent most of the past eighteen months arguing diametrically opposed positions, but his underlying issue was that, as the CEO,

he's felt what he called "a certain sadness" that I, along with other fellow partners, have not appreciated him enough as the founder of our firm and as a mentor figure. I found this particularly interesting because my underlying issue with him is that I don't feel he's appreciated my efforts on the firm's behalf in recent years.

So, I have an idea for an experiment. I'm going to figure out a way to pursue aggressively "getting real" with Sam, so that we can either get on the same page about meeting our expectations of one another or decide once and for all whether, when, and how I should move to another firm.

## Look Through Their Eyes—and See New Possibilities

Once you've verified expectations, these dialogues give you a chance to negotiate ways to better meet each other's expectations and create a more fruitful relationship—in the context of other essential relationships. They allow for an informal assessment of gaps between current performance and some desired state, and how to close them. Of course, some people are going to be more open to this discussion than others. Some will require more give-and-take just to verify expectations before you can talk about finding new ways to meet them.

A fundamental precept of most modern negotiations theorists is this: distinguish underlying interests from stated positions. Expectations are often stated as positions or surface needs. They do not necessarily reflect your stakeholders' deep-seated needs, desires, or fears. Only when you understand a stakeholder's underlying interests can you truly gauge what motivates that person. With this knowledge, you're better able to come up with ideas for new ways of meeting expectations that are good for all your domains. Once you have a good grasp of your shared interests, it then makes sense in your dialogues to test the waters.

For example, let's say that in your stakeholder dialogue with your boss you reach a point where you feel comfortable addressing the prospect of trying a new way to manage boundaries between your work and family life. Going into your dialogue with her, you thought that your boss expected you to be available for phone meetings when you're home in the evening. That is what you took to be her "position." But her "underlying interest"—what she really cares about—is different, which you found out by inquiring about the motivation for her expectations. What you discovered is that she wants to know that she can reach you only if and when she needs you, and that she can rely on your dedicated effort to pursue the goals she's outlined.

By finding this out, you've created an opportunity for exploring other means of satisfying her basic interest in ways that might be good for both of you. You might, for example, say something to her like this:

> I've got this idea. I'd like to try something that I believe will make me more effective in producing results that matter to you—that is, *to not check e-mail between 6 and 9 p.m.* Instead, I'll use that time to focus on other aspects of my life, so that I'll be 100 percent available at other times. This will benefit our business because I'll be more focused and productive and, I believe, happier and health- ier overall. In addition, I will check my e-mail at 9 p.m. to see whether you've sent anything between 6 and 9 p.m., and will respond ASAP. And if it's really an emergency, then I'll have my cell phone available for you to reach me during those hours, as a last resort. How about if we try it for a few weeks and see how this works? If it doesn't, we can go back to the way things were or try something different.

This is a simple example of testing the waters. It proposes new positions for addressing shared interests—yours in bounding that time for your family so that you can feel more focused on work when you're not with them, and your boss's in getting 100 percent focused effort from you whenever you're working and in knowing you're accessible 24/7 if really needed.

Uncovering shared interests—the "elixir of negotiations," as the negotiations scholar Richard Shell calls them—is thus a critical goal for your stakeholder dialogues.[1] It's not easy. We each see the world in our own way, biased by our fears, ignorance, and emotional filters. Getting inside the heads and hearts of your stakeholders is a real leadership challenge. You have to commit to seeing the world through their eyes. Set as your primary goals to listen and understand, even if you don't

## UNCOVER UNDERLYING INTERESTS AND NEW WAYS OF MEETING EXPECTATIONS

To uncover underlying interests and test the waters:

**Ask your stakeholders "why" about their expectations.** Without probing intrusively, express genuine interest in what compels them to want the things they want.

**Use questions to find the basic human need that underlies a stated position.** You are seeking new insight. Your goal is to learn, for the more you understand their interests, the more you will be able to line up your interests with theirs, and, in turn, the more likely it is that they will want to support you.

**Recognize that multiple interests may exist, some of which might be competing.** Understand that there is rarely a clean, black-and-white distinction between the right and wrong choice. Use your judgment to choose among competing interests the one that will best serve the most important long-term needs.

**Focus on a common future.** Common ground that you're both going to tread—this is the road to be paving in your stakeholder dialogues, not the rocky one you might well have been traveling to get there.

Ask what you can do to be a better friend, boss, employee, spouse, sibling, or citizen. Listen carefully to what you hear, restate it in your words, and ask for confirmation. Listening for understanding doesn't commit you to doing anything new; but it does make you more informed about what you might choose to do differently.

Be concrete in what you express to your stakeholders when suggesting changes. Offer specific ideas for action. This helps others to imagine what any change might mean for them.

Ask your stakeholders "why not" about new ways of doing things. Without being too pushy, find a way to inquire about the potential consequences—both good and bad, hoped for and feared —of trying something different than the way things are now.

Now, jot down your further thoughts about how you will approach each dialogue to:

1. Uncover underlying interests and assess how they fit with those of other stakeholders.

2. Discover new ideas for what might be done differently to improve results.

3. Propose an experiment to satisfy your stakeholder's interests in a new, better way.

agree. If you approach your dialogues with a spirit of inquiry—you want to learn, not argue—you will likely open up new pathways.

Just as you develop an overall game plan for each dialogue and how to verify your perceptions about performance expectations, it's useful to think ahead about how you'll aim to uncover underlying interests and explore alternative means of meeting expectations. This next exercise helps you to do this.

If you know what your stakeholders really want, you can offer them what they cannot pass up. Uncovering underlying interests is not manipulation, so long as what you're trying to make happen is in their interests too. You are much less likely to be inhibited by guilt—that source of discouragement that cripples too many people—if you are pursuing a change that you really believe serves your stakeholders' interests as much as it serves yours. This next exercise will help you see the world through their eyes and find common ground.

## GET INSIDE THEIR HEADS AND HEARTS

A role-reversal exercise gives you new ways of understanding the underlying interests of the people who matter to you, from their point of view. In the most useful version of this, you focus on something you'd like to ask someone to do or do differently, a stakeholder you anticipate will say no to your request. Perhaps it's your dreaded stakeholder.

Recruit someone to play the role of you, and you take the role of your stakeholder. When the person playing you asks about the issue, you (playing your stakeholder) say yes and then speculate aloud about *all* the reasons the stakeholder you're role-playing could and *should*—from his or her point of view (not yours)—say yes instead of the no you were anticipating. The person playing the part of you should continue to push, asking for a more detailed explanation and rationale for why you (as your stakeholder) are saying yes to this request.

Mike Miller, an executive MBA student, did this role-playing exercise to prepare for his stakeholder dialogue with his father. He had begun thinking about asking his father to do something big: travel across the country, to California, to help Mike build his new business. Certain his father would refuse, Mike played the role reversal to the hilt in class. He stretched his imagination and came up with a number of reasons why his father could and should say yes (from the point of view of his father's interests), factors he hadn't really thought of in this way before being prodded to do so by the classmate pretending to be Mike. There came a point in the exercise when Mike realized his anticipation of an automatic no was ungrounded. Now he was ready to enter the actual dialogue with a hope of getting a yes, armed with reasons he'd come up with in imagining why yes made sense from his father's point of view. And Mike did get a yes from his father. When this was reported back to our class a few weeks later, a great cheer erupted!

## Finding Common Ground

Through these conversations, it's possible to see more clearly how your performance in one domain affects your performance in other domains. The stakeholder dialogues inform how you might better achieve your goals, how you define your core values, and what you can do to create better alignment between your values and your actions. People have told me that they feel greater self-confidence and satisfaction as a direct result of having these conversations about expectations with their key stakeholders as a set, a system of relationships mutually affecting each other. Before they've done a single experiment, in other words, they are well on the way to producing four-way wins.

Kerry's experience is not uncommon:

I came to these conversations wanting my stakeholders to see how it would help them if I concentrated more on myself, and I learned that they not only are all invested in me but want to see me invest as much in myself as I do in them. This was especially true of my community stakeholders. I expected them to want things of me, but most of them said the same kinds of things: "You do too much for

others." "You work too hard." "You give too much of yourself."
"I would like to see you be as generous to yourself as you are with
your friends." "Sometimes you give so much that I sometimes feel
that I don't do enough in return."

We talked about how investing in myself might benefit all of
my stakeholders. I didn't really need to negotiate as hard as I had
anticipated. And I definitely hadn't given my work stakeholders
enough credit for being flexible and understanding. I learned that
I expect more of myself than they do.

One of my stakeholders even suggested an experiment for me:
to train for a triathlon with some friends and workout partners. I'm
giving it serious thought. It's an experiment that will help me meet
objectives in all domains: I'll be taking care of my health [which will
also make my parents happy] while spending quality time with my
friends—pushing each other and having fun together. Ultimately,
this will help me to feel better and focus more at the office. I think
that knowing I have an obligation to meet people after work will
push me to work efficiently so that I can get home on time and
meet my workout partners!

Within the year, Kerry competed in a triathlon in Canada with two
Total Leadership classmates.

## Build and Restore Trust

Every stakeholder dialogue provides an opportunity to build trust
and to gain support for achieving your goals. Trust—the willingness to
ascribe good intentions to and have confidence in others' words and actions—is the glue that holds relationships together. Leaders depend on
it. Without trust, you don't have the buy-in you need from your stake-

holders. And if they are not on board, your chances of getting important things done are not good.

Business professionals who inspire trust enhance their ability to attract the best workers and keep them. They create a sense of belonging in their organizations and the commitment that comes with that feeling. This, in turn, leads to greater productivity. The bottom line: you want to be seen and known as someone who truly cares about other people and who acts accordingly not only because it feels good but because everyone benefits from doing well for others.

Of course, trust really matters at home, too. Loving relationships are built on the willingness of family members to ascribe good intentions, and the ability to act on them, to each other. People hunger for close connections, and there are ways of cultivating trust with the people closest to you. Speak candidly about the real and important things, show that you care, and trust grows.

Roxanne's dialogues with her children helped her to uncover the interests of her family members in ways she didn't anticipate, and this led to new opportunities to build trust in her most cherished relationships:

My eight-year-old son told me that he thinks I am fun and that he would like to spend our time playing together. He's at the age where he's very focused on video games and playing with his peers, so I was surprised when we talked and he revealed that he valued our time playing together so highly.

My thirteen-year-old daughter, though, told me she feels cheated out of my time and attention, and she's kind of angry with me. She told me that after getting up from bed one night, she found me relaxing on the couch, talking with my husband. She jumped to the conclusion that I always wait until she and her brother go to bed to relax—and therefore become more accessible—and she was hurt and angry that I didn't want to spend time with her. This was a really important perspective for me to understand. When we talked about it, I came to see more clearly why she has been distant lately.

Roxanne's observations show how stakeholder dialogues allow you to learn what people really want from you. Her son gave her a nice surprise, and it got her thinking about how to use her weekend time differently. Her conversation with her daughter is a good example of how intentional dialogues—designed to elucidate expectations—can bring meaningful insights that build stronger connections.

The more you open up to your stakeholders, and the more you get your stakeholders to open up to you, the more they will realize how important the dialogue is to you—*and* to them. They will be able to help you more, the more information you give them. Reciprocal display is ideal: I'll tell you something about me and my interests (such as about my future and how our relationship is essential to it), and then you tell me something about your interests. This path leads to greater trust.

There's value just in letting people know that you care about what they think. Most people appreciate being asked. My bet is that your stakeholders will be impressed to know that you are making a genuine effort to improve your relationship and that you think of them as critical to achieving goals that matter to you.

It's rare that these dialogues result in pressure to do more. To the contrary, they usually result in ideas about how you can reallocate time and energy and, in some cases, reduce pressure in areas that, it turns out, don't matter that much. Quite often these dialogues result in participants feeling less guilty about not doing enough. This opens up the possibility of *actually* doing less of what you thought you were supposed to be doing, which frees up energy for other things you want to do. And if you feel less guilty, you've eliminated a major barrier to leading change.

Jenna learned something about this in her dialogues:

The coworker who asked me to be more demanding shocked me, as did others, by saying that he didn't think I trusted him. I thought we had a very good relationship. But trust came up as a specific issue. One of my team members asked me bluntly why I delegate so few of the things that fill up my schedule and that everyone knows I shouldn't be wasting my time doing. Why don't I trust them, he asked, to do these things they ought to be doing? One of my experiments will be to give my team members greater autonomy. And as I think of it, it sure will be nice to be freed from some of the tasks I'm doing now. I'll be able to concentrate on some more strategic issues for our group.

Trust is a fragile commodity, and in a stakeholder dialogue there are a few rules that have proven effective in dealing with broken trust. The first has to do with honoring perceptions. Put simply, if you or your stakeholder sees trust as broken, then it's broken. There is no point in arguing *whether* the break is real. The perception of broken trust is what matters—and if the relationship is worth saving, it must be repaired. Assume that if you have accurately identified your stakeholders, and they are indeed the most important people in each of your life domains, then repairing broken trust is a priority.

How do you repair broken trust? It begins with an exploration of where the break occurred, acceptance of the breach, and a sincere apology. You need to acknowledge that broken trust has had a negative impact on your relationship, and that this is a problem. Explain actions that may have led to the break, but do not justify them defensively. Help the other person see what led you to make the choice you made, but remember not to make this into an argument. The most important thing is to indicate—so that he or she understands well—your willingness to do what it takes to make the repair because the relationship matters to you and your future.

### Start Talking!

Just as great performers spend most of their time training, preparation is invaluable for your stakeholder dialogues. These heart-to-hearts are not easy, despite what most participants say after the fact. You've built your foundation for taking action, but so far you've not dealt directly with other people. Now you will, and it can be tough.

All kinds of things make people feel uneasy as they gear up. Some worry that they may come across as trying to pull something over on, for instance, their parents. Some are sure that they can't have a meaningful dialogue with their young children. But you've now prepared yourself for these conversations; they will be worthwhile, and once they're done, you'll have plenty of great material to work with in designing experiments.

Practicing the Total Leadership method means respecting the whole person—connecting with your people. You must be genuinely curious about them. Adopt a spirit of inquiry, of discovery. Try not to be defensive. Identify the interests underlying their expectations and relentlessly search for how, why, and where those interests fit well with all the others that matter to you.

## TALK, TAKE NOTES, AND REFLECT

Having done the three other exercises in this chapter and prepared for each dialogue, find the right setting and make them happen. It's best to do them all within the span of a couple of weeks. This enhances your ability to see the whole for the parts.

After each one, take a few notes, including on the following:

- What surprises, if any, emerged from the conversation?

- What became of any concerns you had going into this dialogue?

- What new insights do you have about how your different domains affect each other?

- What new ideas for innovation came to mind?

Now, after you've completed all your stakeholder dialogues, take some time to read through your notes and reflect on what you've learned. Write a page or so answering these questions:

- Where is there compatibility among what your stakeholders expect of you?

- Where is there conflict (in addition to competition for your time) among what your stakeholders expect of you?

- What changes can you imagine making that will enhance compatibility, reduce conflict, and improve your performance and satisfaction in all domains?

This is a good time to talk to your coaches or trusted advisers about your observations and ideas.

# PART III

# BE INNOVATIVE
## Act with Creativity

## CHAPTER 6

# Design Experiments

T O BE INNOVATIVE by acting with creativity is to adapt to new circumstances with confidence. Doing so keeps you vital, and effective leaders are continually rethinking the way things get done while focusing on results. It takes courage to experiment to better meet the expectations of people who depend on you. And using the insights you've gained from all the work you've done so far, in this part of the book you'll practice how to do this by tackling the challenge of designing and implementing smart experiments intended to produce benefits for your work, your home, your community, and your self— four-way wins—just as Ismail Hashemi did.

Ismail is fifty years old and lives in the Washington, D.C., area. He is an intense man whose gaze when fixed upon you is searing. His frizzy hair is thinning, but he's always impeccably dressed in Italian sweaters or custom-tailored suits. Having grown up in an affluent family in the Middle East, Ismail never really struggled for what he needed, but there came a point in his life when his family's good fortunes collapsed, and he found himself—virtually overnight—going from freshly minted college graduate with the luxury of taking time to "find himself" to someone with little money and nowhere to turn. He learned to survive and create his own opportunities, entering the business world, falling in love, and marrying. His engineering services company prospered. He had twin boys relatively late in life and found himself changed by their birth. His eyes tear up when he speaks about his children.

Ismail said that he signed up for my Total Leadership course to become more proactive and less of a procrastinator. He also wanted to find an answer to a burning question:

> What can I do to strengthen my business, to do things better at work, and to be a better father and husband? My business is absorbing huge amounts of my time and energy, both physical and emotional. I feel like I'm neglecting my family, but I am not sure what I can do about it. I have seen people drop out of business because they felt they weren't living up to things at home. More often, I have seen people fall into business so far that they don't even recognize a problem outside that realm. Increasingly, I am finding that my focus on work makes me feel distant from my wife and kids.
>
> Even with all my business achievements, and even though I am making a large amount of money, I feel that something is missing, that I'm not living up to my own expectations—even if I'm not completely sure what these are. Sometimes, I even feel resentment toward myself for the choices I make. I can't really make sense of that.

These were the goals he wrote about at the start (as you did in chapter 1). Yet he said he was "afraid procrastination may prevent me from achieving the results I am hoping to gain." By the time he was ready to start designing experiments, Ismail had gotten more real: he took a look at his life and clarified what was important. He had gotten more whole:

he had listened to the voices of his inner circle and saw how the branches of his life were connected. His next step was to get more innovative and create experiments to produce four-way wins:

> I've got experiments lined up that should hit all four domains. In one, I'm going to get my business partners to make a change in the way our company operates. To make it work, we're going to employ smart phones—a new technology for us—which I'll try to use with my wife, too. In another, I'm going to set aside special time with my kids, scheduled in advance and held sacrosanct, and for the church meetings I've been missing. In making these changes, I'm sure I'll feel less conflicted and better about myself.

Like Ismail, once you've completed the previous chapters, you're ready to plan experiments to score four-way wins—and to learn how to be a better leader and have a richer life by doing so. Whether or not you went into your stakeholder dialogues with ideas for experiments already in mind, you may have tested their feasibility in these discussions. Now it's time to select the most promising opportunities, think through your game plan, specify your goals, and devise means for tracking progress. Then: action!

## Types of Total Leadership Experiments

A Total Leadership experiment is a planned change—something new that's a doable stretch. It is deliberately aimed at making life demonstrably better in all four domains, founded on what you've learned so far. While aiming to make things better in each domain, an experiment's main action can take place in but a *single domain* and have *indirect benefits* in other domains (e.g., changing jobs improves your self-esteem and makes you a better father and friend), or it can occur in *multiple domains* simultaneously and so have *direct impact* on all of them (e.g., training with your kids for a marathon that raises funds for a charity sponsored by your company). Either way, by direct or indirect impact, achieving a four-way win is the purpose of a Total Leadership experiment.

Before reviewing some guidelines for how to think about yours, let's consider the different kinds of experiments. The paths taken by Total Leadership participants are as many as there are participants. My research team has found, however, after scouring detailed descriptions of hundreds of experiments, that there are generic types. In practice, though, most experiments are best described as a combination or *hybrid* of more than one of these types. A quick review will show you the range of experiments that are possible and help you come up with ones that are best suited for your situation.

> **Tracking and Reflecting** experiments involve keeping a record of activities, thoughts, and feelings to assess progress on goals. This can increase self-awareness, help maintain priorities and, in turn, clarify what's important. One participant, an insurance company executive who was also an amateur athlete, began a monthly log of his performance in his home and community domains, which he'd identified as problematic. He came to notice that he had failed to quantify his level of effort in these areas, despite having learned from sports how important it is to track progress.

> **Planning and Organizing** experiments involve taking new actions designed to use time better and plan for the future. This might involve using a new technology for organizing, or creating "to do" lists that involve all life domains, or engaging in a new form of planning with your family. One Total Leadership participant, a principal in a management consulting firm, designed an experiment to set a few "must keep" dates with his wife and his children, which he treated not just as appointments on his calendar but as a "deliberate attempt to define things better with stakeholders" at work and at home.

**Rejuvenating and Restoring** experiments involve attending to body, mind, and spirit so that tasks are undertaken with renewed power and focus on top priorities. The self domain is the easiest one to ignore: you can always cancel an "appointment" you make for yourself without risking any social repercussions. Perhaps this is why these experiments are so popular. Engaging in a regular program of exercise is a common kind of restorative experiment. One Total Leadership participant, a high-tech marketing executive, experimented with arriving at work earlier so she could leave earlier and spend the evening either at the gym or with friends. This motivated her to be more productive during the day and to meet deadlines she set for getting out of the office.

**Appreciating and Caring** experiments involve having fun with people, caring for others, and appreciating relationships. Bonding at a basic human level respects the whole person and increases trust. Some Total Leadership participants experiment by doing things with coworkers outside of work. A supervisor of lab technicians at a chemical company experimented by organizing more social events for coworkers, to "build morale and work as a team better." She saw this as a way to create greater efficiency at the office, but also as a way for everyone to carve out time for enriching nonwork activities.

**Focusing and Concentrating** experiments involve efforts to be physically or psychologically present when needed by key stakeholders. Sometimes this means saying no to certain opportunities in order to be accessible to people. When Mike Cohen, a pharmaceutical sales manager, learned from his stakeholder assessments that he was spending too much time each day at work on "valueless" activities, he set out to delegate more while improving his ability to say no to requests for his time. It wasn't easy, but this resulted in his spending less time at home each evening on work-related tasks and more time on doing things around the house with and for his wife. His performance at work actually went up.

**Revealing and Engaging** experiments involve sharing more of yourself with others—and listening to them—so they can better understand your values and support the steps you want to take toward your leadership vision. Effective leaders continually nurture connections. An executive MBA student with retired parents living in India had given up on talking to them about his work and its challenges. But he realized that his father, who had worked for AT&T in the United States for twenty-six years, might have much to offer. It was only the "times and nomenclature" that had changed. By communicating with his parents, he made them more a part of his life and reaped benefits at work from his father's years of experience.

**Time-shifting and Re-placing** experiments involve working remotely or during different hours to increase flexibility and efficiency in different domains. These experiments often make you question traditional assumptions about work methods. One Total Leadership participant, a sales director for a global cement producer, tried stationing himself at his local public library while tethered online to the office, one day per week, to eliminate his very long commute. He had to break away from the culture of a company that didn't traditionally support employees working remotely to make this change, which, he said, turned out to "benefit everyone."

**Delegating and Developing** experiments involve reallocating tasks in ways that increase trust, free up time, and develop skills, often through working smarter by reducing low-priority activities. One participant, an investment banker, assigned more responsibility for data analysis and report writing to her team. This yielded more time for her other projects while presenting her staff with a chance to learn new competencies. Her inability to accomplish these other projects had been weighing heavily on her. By making this change, she was now more available for her family, her friends, and her workouts at the gym.

**Exploring and Venturing** experiments involve taking steps toward starting a new job, career, or activity that allows you to better fit your actions with your core values and your leadership vision. A financial services executive had set out in his leadership vision that he wanted to run a company and be more involved in the life of his local community. So he joined a municipal board, where he cultivated his leadership skills. First, though, he talked with the director of his firm's public-service foundation; together they crafted a training plan to prepare him for board membership. The experiment helped him move a bit further on his "quest to become a CEO."

In short, there are all kinds of possibilities! Let's develop specific ideas for yours, plan them out, and get them started.

## Generating Ideas for Experiments

Your experiments must aim to produce benefits in all domains, and hopefully they will. Whether or not you actually end up scoring four-way wins, however, the more important long-term outcome is this: smart experiments foster knowledge about how to do so in the future. You become better able to lead and enrich your life by practicing how to create mutual value among domains, by mobilizing support for achieving worthwhile goals and by reflecting on what actually happens. Here are some guidelines for contemplating the possibilities:

*Experiment with where, when, and how you
get things done.*

Use your experiments as opportunities—even if they are simple
ones—for you and others to try getting things done from a total life perspective. Aim to make things easier by rethinking the way you get things
done now.

*Use your organization.*

Involve as much of your work organization as possible. (If you don't
go to an office, whether you're between jobs, in school, or work at home,
think about this in a way that is relevant for your situation.) While an experiment might affect people beyond your immediate circle, however,
focus your action on what you can influence and control.

*Enlist stakeholders.*

Each of your experiments is a leadership challenge, a stretch that
will naturally encounter some resistance (what important changes don't?).
You'll need to invite key stakeholders to help you. With your core values
and your leadership vision as foundations, take a stand for changes that
serve collective interests.

*Manage boundaries to focus better and to pay attention.*

In gaining a more refined picture of the expectations surrounding
you, you've probably realized that the time you spend is not the same as
the attention you devote to other people and activities. To focus attention intelligently is to manage the shifting, ever-more-permeable boundaries between domains. New media make the boundaries harder to hold,
but also provide us with tools we can use to make life easier. Look at
what makes sense for you in a given situation.

Sometimes opening the boundaries to merge domains will allow you
to better focus on what's worthwhile. You might conduct an experiment

that *combines* domains, bringing activities from different parts of your life together. Exercising with your spouse combines your self and home domains; inviting coworkers to your home for a dinner you've cooked combines your work, home, and self domains. Combining also includes discussing issues from one domain with stakeholders in another domain, such as if you were to talk about work with your family to gain their understanding or solicit advice. You are combining when you use skills from one domain in another, or when you rethink how activity in one domain affects other domains. So, for example, you might experiment with how you can show your employees how their work in your company contributes to making the world a better place. Combining domains makes the boundaries between domains more permeable.

On the other hand, experiments that aim to *segment domains* encourage people and activities from different parts of your life to remain separate—so that you can focus better. For instance, you might decide not to answer phone calls from work when you're at home, or not take personal calls at the office. You might decide that you will keep work and home separate by avoiding any discussion about what happened at the office during family dinner. Some bounding experiments involve behavioral changes, such as deciding consciously not to use behaviors that you would exhibit at work when dealing with intimate companions. If you're a management consultant used to aggressive problem solving with clients, for example, you may find yourself doing this more and more with close friends, who may want you simply as a confidante—a sympathetic ear, a nonjudgmental pal, someone able to hold their pain—rather than as a hard-driving business associate.

A central feature of the Total Leadership approach is the intentional focus on what and who matters most—clarifying what's important, both in the big picture, by acting in accord with your core values, and in the here and now, as part of (and in spite of) the everyday hustle and bustle. But the ability to pay attention seems to be getting harder every day. Many business professionals feel overwhelmed, and so it's common to hear the cry "Release me from the bonds of digital slavery!" Just about everyone is struggling with the incessant demands wrought by their 24/7 availability online. In response to this problem, many Total Leadership participants design their experiments to become better able to pay attention to the people who need them at the time when they are so needed.

For some, this requires practicing the art of what I call "interruptability"—being able to turn your full attention from one person or task to another in a diplomatic way. For others, it means practice in giving full attention by being both psychologically and physically present. In one of her experiments, for example, a physician worked on keeping her eyes on the residents she trained as she talked with them as a supervisor.

As Jeff Greenhaus and I found in our research, focused attention is a critical variable in determining whether you're able to integrate the different parts of your life. Time is not so much the issue as is the ability to pay attention to what matters, when it matters. Psychological interference of one domain on another is what gives us grief: worrying about work when you're with your children, or vice versa, for example.

Some people think that the focusing of your complete attention on someone else is an act of grace. Others think of it as "being here now" or "in the moment" or "in the flow of life." Indeed, living in the present while simultaneously being mindful of the past and of the future is for many people a central aim of spiritual growth. The Sabbath, what theologian Abraham Joshua Heschel calls an "architecture of time," is a way people have devised to focus on the most important things in life, bounding one day in seven for these purposes.[1] By observing the Sabbath, one carries into the prosaic routines of one's workdays a transcendent appreciation for the gift of life, of one's precious, fleeting time on earth. I'm not advocating for Sabbath observance and all that entails. Rather, I'm pointing out that such ritual observances in many religious traditions compel people to take time for rejuvenation, reflection, and rest. It's useful to consider whether such practices might be helpful, and whether your experiments aid your development of them.

> ## IDENTIFY POSSIBLE FOUR-WAY WINS
>
> Start by brainstorming. In light of what you've learned from everything you've done in this book, what could you try that would produce some benefit for each of your four domains? What could you do now in your real world during a trial period of, say, a month or so?
>
> Don't worry about obstacles. We'll get to those shortly. Just open your mind to what's possible and compose a list of as many as you can, describing what you would do for each experiment in a sentence or two. Take your time to gather up a pocketful of prospects.

### How Jenna and Roxanne Thought About Their Experiments

In Jenna's dialogue with her boss, she was "shocked" to learn that he thought of her as a sister and cared tremendously about her personal happiness. Jenna also talked to her direct reports, who asked her to push them harder and delegate more. On the home front, she had just learned that her father had been diagnosed with cancer. She concluded that the experiment that would most benefit all domains was to work fewer hours and perhaps even take an unpaid leave from work to spend more time with her father.

I realized that to accomplish this successfully, I would need to involve my manager and explain to the people I manage why I would be doing this. I see now that I have to show them how it will benefit them. For one thing, this is an opportunity for me to delegate, to give them expanded responsibilities, which in turn will expose them to more experiences as they advance in their careers.

At first I thought this innovation would compromise my position in my firm, but I've come to realize that it could actually be an opportunity to stretch my leadership skills. I'll have to find new ways of staying close to my peers while working remotely. With my direct reports, I'll have to try delegating more while making sure that their careers continue to develop with these expanded responsibilities. And I'll have to make sure I keep my boss in the loop. Everyone has to know the level, and the impact, of the work I'm doing.

Jenna was homing in on how her experiment could improve her performance and win results in multiple domains. She would spend more time with her father without feeling guilty about not being at work, and would be better able to communicate with him and even take walks together. She would feel better about herself and the choices she makes as to where she spends her time. And at work she would feel more secure in her position without the guilt that can often come with taking time away from the office.

She wouldn't worry about what her direct reports and manager thought, because she would have their buy-in. This is part of the beauty of sharing goals with your stakeholders. What you need and want to accomplish goes from secrets enshrouded in unnecessary mystery to public topics that people can help you with.

Roxanne Pappas-Grant based the design of one of her experiments on what she'd learned in talking with her two kids, ages thirteen and eight.

I see an important opportunity on weekend nights—one I've been squandering. Instead of watching my daughter read a book and looking on as my son plays his Game Boy, I'm going to figure out how to shift our interactions to something more engaging, something that will take full advantage of our time together. If I do this right, it will relieve the pressure on less-convenient weeknights. And, it will make me feel less pressure at work. I'll be changing what I do in my downtime (my self domain) to enhance my family life. Less stress at home will allow me to focus better when I'm working. Then I can set some goals for better results. Everyone gains—me, my kids, and my business partners.

Even as she began to formulate her experiment, however, Roxanne could already see the challenges she would face.

If we're going to have a Friday night family activity, I'm going to have to make sure to get home on time. I've always been terrible about leaving work at a reasonable hour on Fridays, so I'm really going to have to be more of a leader at work and get people at work involved in some way. I'll have to show them that my leaving by a certain time on Fridays benefits them, too.

Of course I'll need my husband to support these activities with the family. And I'll need some way to see how this is creating better results at work. I'm going to ask my team what they think about how to measure the impact on our performance.

## CHOOSE THE MOST PROMISING

On the basis of your responses to the previous exercise, narrow your list down to the three most promising by reviewing which will:

- Give you the best overall return on your investment
- Be the most costly to you if you *don't* do it
- Allow you to practice the skills you most want to develop
- Be the most fun by having you do more of what you want to be doing
- Move you most directly toward your leadership vision

Three is a good number. Typically, two experiments turn out more or less as planned, and one goes haywire. It is unlikely that they will go as planned, but investments in smartly designed experiments almost always pay off. The "failure" can hold the greatest value, as it can provide the most memorable opportunity for learning. Keep in mind, too, that you can always change your plans for experiments as new information and opportunities arise.

### The Ultimate Experiment

An experiment I recently chose was to contribute to building a start-up, an Ultimate Frisbee club for our high school. We call ourselves Babaganouj—a name coined by one of the teenagers—and one of our slogans is "Spread the love!" The idea for this experiment emerged when one of my sons, Gabriel, then seventeen, was playing Ultimate in a local summer league. I watched from the sidelines with his brother, Harry, who was about to enter his sophomore year and was too young for league play. Both are wildly enthusiastic about this wonderful sport, which is self-refereed and governed by a spirit of mutual respect and discovery. (At tournaments, awards are given not just to the teams that win games but also to those that best show this spirit.)

I viewed this as a hybrid experiment that combined domains and had elements of three types: rejuvenating and restoring (playing the game), exploring and venturing (starting a new club), and appreciating and caring (doing fun stuff to deepen connections with my children). My efforts to help launch Babaganouj touch all four of my domains, three of them directly. On the home front, I'm doing something with my children, and it's something they like. In my community, I'm helping to build an organization that now serves many children. And for my health, training with them is contributing to my well-being. The indirect effects are with my work and career; I'm learning about the challenges of a start-up while writing and talking about this experiment in my teaching.

As for results, in addition to improving my physical health, spending high-quality time with my sons while seeing them grow, and learning more about influence in volunteer organizations, I've contributed to building a club we hope will last for a long time—we've now got over fifty regular members (way more than the football team!), including a boy's team, a girl's team, and a junior varsity squad. We set out to be recognized as an official club of the school, and now we are. We set a goal of playing in the state championship tournament, and did, placing fifth in our first year. And we've won a coveted "spirit" award at more than one of our tournaments. Not only do the students love it, numerous parents have said that this team was a highlight of their child's high school experience.

At our year-end team party, our faculty sponsor/coach said something that resonates well with the aims of this book: the experience of Babaganouj had changed the way she feels about her career. For the first

## SET YOUR GAME PLANS

Think through your game plan for each experiment. To do so, write notes on your thoughts about each of the issues below.

I recommend a separate game plan for each of your experiments to address:

- How this experiment follows each of the guidelines described earlier in this chapter

- What you hope to learn from it, on the basis of what you've done in previous chapters

- How you intend to capture value from one domain and transfer it to others

- What assistance or advice you need to implement this experiment

- What obstacles you will need to overcome to implement this experiment

- What ways this initiative is innovative—how it's new, for you

If you are working with a coach, discuss your game plan together. You might want to get ideas from others, too, at www.totalleadership.org or elsewhere.

time in a long while, she told our happy gathering, she was feeling sad (rather than relieved) at the end of the school year, knowing that she wouldn't have these incredible kids stopping by her office to talk about Ultimate.

Before I began to take small steps to move this promising idea forward, I didn't think much about the time it would end up consuming. I sensed that it was a good idea because it was important to my family and I could help make it successful for them and for our community. This experiment showed me once again that when you try to do something you believe in for people whom you care about deeply, then there's a decent chance your work will benefit as you become a stronger person because of the effort, exercising the muscles of your soul.

## Win Small, Win Smart

Your experiments don't have to be massive, all-encompassing shifts in the way you live. Such designs usually fail because they're just too much to handle. The best experiments provide an opportunity for you to try new ways of getting things done while minimizing the inevitable risks associated with change. Roxanne was concerned about one of her ideas:

> I want to shift from my heavy reliance on face-to-face communication in favor of e-mail and other approaches. In truth, I have such a strong preference for face-to-face interaction—particularly with individuals like my boss—that I really have to force myself to use e-mail. I'm concerned about being misinterpreted in e-mail, and I've been having difficulty getting over this mental barrier.

Roxanne overcame this hurdle by taking the relatively small risk of trusting just one or two people to become e-mail correspondents, for starters. By taking these "baby steps," incrementally moving forward in her new chosen direction, Roxanne exploited the power of small wins, a practical means for creating big change.

Small wins are *doable*. When you undertake something that you know is in your control to try, it's easier to overcome the fear of failure. I find this analogy useful, even if extreme: how does the prisoner of war remain sane and survive? He copes by narrowing his scope, his focus, his range of discretionary action, to that which he can control. If he has no control over his physical environment and he can control only what's in his mind, then he focuses there. Of course, you have more options than he does. And you have more discretion—more control over decisions about whether you may try something new—than you might have thought. Perhaps you found this out when you talked about expectations in your stakeholder dialogues and discovered that people expect less of you than you had imagined.

When you adopt the small-wins approach to leading change, you remain grounded in measurable actions. You have a greater sense of control over what happens, and so it becomes safer to experiment. The metrics you will establish for your experiments later in this chapter will provide the data you'll need to gauge what's working. Metrics help you improve performance by showing how you need to adjust your actions. People learn leadership by doing it, by taking action to change things, and then reflecting on the experience to discover insights about what works and what doesn't. You can't do this unless you have information about the impact of your actions.

As a result of changes you make, you start to see the effects—and with data you can demonstrate that things really are better. This helps build support from others while inspiring you to continue despite any initial misgivings. Small wins build commitment and the will to proceed further. Success breeds success. When people see you trying to make things better, they get excited about the direction you're moving toward. The more success you demonstrate, the less resistance arises.

Another benefit of the small-wins approach is that it opens doors otherwise closed. When introducing a new initiative, you can say to the people from whom you need support, "Let's just try this. If it doesn't

work, we'll go back to the old way or try something different." By framing an experiment as a trial, you reduce resistance because people are
more likely to try something new if they know it's not permanent and if
they have control over deciding whether the experiment is working, according to *their* performance expectations.

But don't get hung up on the word *small*. This isn't about the scope or
importance of the changes you eventually make. Large-scale change is
based on having a big idea but then taking small steps toward it. For instance, the idea for the Ismail's first experiment was, as he described it, to
"restructure my company and my role in it"—nothing small about that.
The actual first steps he took, however, *were* small and achievable. He
began to change some reporting relationships. And he introduced a new
technology to spur new patterns of communication and decision making.
Today Ismail describes his experiments as "a true testament to the idea of
winning the small battles and letting the war be won as a result."

## The Scorecard—Specific Goals and Metrics

Having thought through your game plan for your experiments, you
can now devise a scorecard for each one that specifies your goals and
gives you the information you'll need to assess both when you've reached
them and your progress in moving toward them.

### *Defining Your Goals for Each Domain*

Worthwhile goals have real personal meaning, are specific, and are
moderately difficult. The fundamental issue to be thinking about here is
how the intended benefits of your innovations propel you further toward
being the kind of leader you want to become and the world you want to
live in. More specifically, what you'll write on your scorecard is how your
experiment is designed to make things better in all domains.

## CREATE SCORECARD—GOALS

A blank scorecard for each of your experiments is shown below. In this and the next exercise, I'll show you how to complete it. Either make a few copies of it, or fashion something like this scorecard elsewhere for your use with each of your experiments. (Visit www.totalleadership.org for more ideas.)

Certain types of experiments combine logically as a single, coherent whole. But others do not: doing exercise daily, having dinner with your family, and changing your work hours—these three are not a single experiment and are best thought of as separate. Try to avoid the temptation to list a hodgepodge of different experiments as a single hybrid. Differentiate such actions and design them as separate experiments. You'll learn more from them if you do so. Also, you might find that your initial ideas for an experiment are too broad or too vague. If so, break the plan down into two or more specific experiments that you can implement now.

First, write a brief description of this experiment at the top of the page. Then record your goals for each domain in the first column. Each of the four domains must have an intended benefit that is meaningful to the relevant stakeholders in that domain. This might require a stretch because the benefits might be indirect or they might not be seen until sometime in the future. Do your best to come up with at least one goal for each domain.

**Experiment Scorecard—Goals and Metrics**

**Experiment:**

|  | Goal: Intended Impact | Results Metrics | Action Metrics |
|---|---|---|---|
| Work |  |  |  |
| Home |  |  |  |
| Community |  |  |  |
| Self |  |  |  |

## Devising Your Metrics

You are experimenting, like a scientist. The only way to fail with an experiment is to fail to learn from it. Metrics not only help you determine whether you hit specific targets; they also provide a basis for learning. We learn from what we measure, and so you need data to learn what works and what doesn't. No doubt, it's better to achieve the results you are after than to fall short, yet it's important to remember that just hitting targets does not in itself advance you toward the leader you want to become. That requires *learning*, which occurs when you draw insights from your experience, whether success or failure.

Establishing a set of reliable metrics gives you tools to measure both actions and results. *Action metrics* allow you to track progress, which will in turn increase the odds that you actually achieve your goals. *Results metrics* can help you enlist support by showing how investments in your experiments yield valuable returns not just for you but also for your key stakeholders. They answer this: what would be the proof that with my experiment I have made things better?

Designing metrics that are relevant for your particular experiments requires some creativity. Whether they refer to results or actions, metrics can vary along a number of dimensions.

Metrics can be *objective* or *subjective*. Objective metrics are those that can be determined impartially; any observer privy to your actions or results would rate you the same way on an objective metric. Subjective metrics, in contrast, are based on perceptions. Both *can* be useful; what's important is to employ metrics that *are* useful. So, as you decide whether to set an objective or subjective measure, consider the pros and cons of each type and choose metrics that are easy to manage and motivating to you. If you decide to collect feedback from others—a subjective metric—you can reduce the inherent bias by increasing the number of people providing feedback.

Metrics can be *frequently* or *intermittently observed*. Results are measured at the end of a defined experimental period. Action metrics, though, can be measured more frequently, as often as you see fit. What's the right frequency? Measuring too often is burdensome. Not measuring frequently enough can cause you to lose focus. Consider how often it makes sense to track yourself, and make this explicit on your scorecard. Think about how long you will be able to remember your actions. For example, if you were to go on a diet to improve performance in all domains, and monitoring food intake was an important action metric, would you be able to remember what you ate two days ago? Metrics that can be used at many stages are valuable for tracking progress and keeping you on top of your experiments. They help raise awareness of changes that may need to be made during the course of the experiment.

Your metrics can be *reported by yourself* or *by someone else*. In many cases, you might be the only person able to keep track of your actions, especially when they are focused internally (e.g., meditating). In other cases, though, it may be best to rely on the observations of others, as, for example, when you want to assess how grumpy you are. It can be hard for us to see certain behaviors in ourselves that we want to change, and it's easy to ignore or just not see the effects we have on others. Asking others to report their perceptions of your actions and attitudes is often valuable.

Metrics can be *quantitative* or *qualitative*. Will you use numbers or words to track your performance? Keeping a diary of your thoughts or feelings might be appropriate in some cases, while it may be more effective to assign numerical values in your metrics in other cases. Numbers can reflect concrete behaviors or outcomes, such as the number of phone calls you made during a given week, how many pounds you lost, or how much money you saved. Numbers can also be used to quantify less concrete thoughts and feelings. For example, rather than writing down how satisfied you are, you could gauge your satisfaction on a numerical scale.

Metrics can be *specific* or *general*. A metric focused on delegating work could be written as whether you delegate work to others, whether you delegate work to others each week, or how many times each week you delegate your report-writing duties to others. Make your metrics as specific as possible with consideration for the level of specificity that's appropriate to your needs.

### Examples of Results Metrics

Results metrics are measures that you design to fit your experiment to produce data on whether you actually produce a four-way win. Here are some examples of customized results metrics that have been used by past participants in Total Leadership, listed by domain.

WORK

- Did we improve ratings from customers about the quality of our service?

- Did we avoid cost by reducing travel and, if so, by how much?

HOME

- Did I have fewer arguments per day with my kids?

- Did I talk with my mother each week, and does she report feeling closer to me?

COMMUNITY

- Did I show up each week at the teen center and do three hours of volunteer work?

- Did I go through at least one box of old children's books in the attic and drop off the good ones at the women's shelter?

SELF

- Did I increase my level of strength, adding five push-ups per week until I can do fifty?

- Did I speak in public at least twice each month, in whatever forum I could find?

### Examples of Action Metrics

Below are examples of action metrics for various types of experiments. Some are big in scope, some are small. Remember, they are only examples; your success hinges on developing metrics that are right for you and relevant for your experiments.

TRACKING AND REFLECTING

- How often do I sacrifice planned activities for another obligation?

- Are my "to do" items done within a week of being added to the list?

PLANNING AND ORGANIZING

- How many missed appointments and double bookings did I have in a week?

- How many fifteen-minute intervals did I spend in planning (goal = one per business day)?

REJUVENATING AND RESTORING

- How many visits to the gym did I make this week?

- How much sleep did I get each night?

APPRECIATING AND CARING

- How many days did I eat lunch away from my desk with others?

- How many hours did I spend with my kids last week?

## FOCUSING AND CONCENTRATING

- How many times did I take work home with me on nights and/or weekends?

- Did I have conversations in which I did nothing else but stay engaged?

## REVEALING AND ENGAGING

- From people I've not communicated with in months, how many e-mails did I receive?

- Did I increase time spent in face-to-face conversation with family by five hours per week?

## TIME-SHIFTING AND RE-PLACING

- How many hours did I work remotely?

- What percent of Tuesday and Thursday nights was I home on time for dinner?

## DELEGATING AND DEVELOPING

- Did I reduce my client load by at least one per week?

- Did I delegate two household chores per month to someone else?

## EXPLORING AND VENTURING

- Did I write some part of my new book every day?

- How many new recipes did I try for the menu for my future restaurant?

## CREATE SCORECARD METRICS

Record your results and action metrics for each domain in the second and third columns, respectively. First, in the middle column of the scorecard, for each intended benefit record how you will measure whether the goal has been achieved. Then, in the last column, indicate how you'll measure the actions you'll take in implementing your experiment.

## Mustering the Will to Try Something New

Your game plans and scorecards are in place. Do you have the will to move forward? Intentional changes often get stalled not for lack of a great idea, but for the failure to act. There are three main reasons. Sometimes, people are unwilling to experiment out of *fear*. For instance, you may not advocate for a flexible work arrangement, fearing that you will be seen as less than committed. You may simply fear being told no. In other situations, you might stay with the status quo because *guilt* prevents you from trying a new way of getting things done; you don't want to be self-serving. And then there's *ignorance* or lack of imagination: you may be unaware that there actually *are* other ways to do things.

Anything new is bound to provoke some anxiety and uncertainty. How do you overcome these inhibitions so that you can vigorously carry out your experiments? It starts with the right frame of mind. You need a good idea that you believe in, *and* you must get others to believe in that idea and see how it's good for them. Obstacles are everywhere if you're trying something meaningful, and they can be particularly daunting in the work domain, where careers are on the line. This amplifies the need for you to be skillful in adapting.

You're going to confront unknowns when you cut new paths. Persisting in the face of resistance—having the courage to lead change—

derives from having a sense of purpose, taking intelligent risks, and knowing how to adjust quickly. It comes from knowing that you're contributing to the success of others, building stronger connections among others, and increasing everyone's sense of belonging to something *bigger*. "You can't succeed with experiments without the involvement and support of others," said André, as he began to act on his plans. And he is right on target.

How to get going and make something new stick is the subject to which we now turn.

## CHAPTER 7

# Bring Others Along with You

I N CHAPTER 6, you read about how the small-wins approach to leading change reduces resistance and builds confidence, how it helps you to get past the "they won't let me" problem that too often hampers change. In this chapter, you'll find additional guidance on how to marshal your resolve by drawing on insights you've generated about acting with authenticity and integrity. And you'll learn more about how to gain real commitment from the people around you and how useful it is to go further, taking a measure of the world beyond your immediate circle: doing so can be inspiring as you start to move forward with your experiments.

André's stakeholder dialogues had suggested an experiment that would move him closer to the leadership vision he had described at the beginning of his Total Leadership journey. André had envisioned creating a nationwide chain of high-end salons predominantly serving black women. As a first step, he imagined an online community designed to promote skills development, financial security, and business ownership among independent black stylists and salon owners. He realized that in taking this first step, he would create a new sector in his work domain—his own business.

In his conversations with his wife, André learned that she didn't care that much about the amount of money he made. She thought his financial expectations were "too extreme." She just wanted to be comfortable, and to be with him more often.

This experiment—creating an online community—will allow me to spend more time with my wife in a meaningful endeavor that taps our mutual passions and interests. Plus, my wife wants to become more computer savvy.

He also realized, in his stakeholder analyses and dialogues, how important it was for him to be doing something now about contributing, by way of his work, to something bigger than just the immediate circle of his family.

I defined members of the black community in general as key stakeholders. I'm motivated by group empowerment and the desire to generate wealth and self-sufficiency for this community. My experiment immediately boosts my engagement with these stakeholders. My wife expressed concern about my participation in community-building activities at the expense of family time, so our joint focus on this project should mitigate this concern. I'm bringing her into it.

His experiment shows his new level of understanding about how his different domains tie together as a system. He was enthusiastic about the changes he was embarking on as he began to move forward, but also a bit daunted as a new reality came into view, particularly in relation to

Marta: "I was a bit uneasy about entering into a working relationship with her. What if it failed? What if she didn't perform to expectations? What if she didn't believe in me and my vision?"

There are bound to be all kinds of what-ifs and resistance when you are starting something. If not dealt with effectively, they will destroy your initiative. In this chapter, then, as you get going on your experiments, we'll explore further how to find the courage to overcome the obstacles, both internal and external, that leaders face when trying to create sustainable change in their worlds.

## Get in the Game!

The small-wins approach is effective because you make a well-considered move, get quick feedback on its impact, use this information to make adjustments to better meet the needs of the people around you, and so improve your chances of everyone ending up as winners. If you haven't yet, then now's the time to take those first steps. And even as you're just getting started, it's useful to be attuned to those affected by your actions to see how it's going for them and assess whether to modify your actions in light of what's working and what's not.

When you're implementing your experiments, expect the unexpected, and be ready to adjust according to what you learn from the facts on the ground. You can't foresee all the ways in which your interests will interact with the interests of the people around you. You're going to run into things you didn't see before. For instance, let's say you decide to have a regular weekend bicycle ride with your kids, and then you find out that they're not actually as available as you thought they were. Turns out that they have their *own* schedules, with commitments you didn't know about. So you have to adjust and adapt. Perhaps rather than bringing your daughter along on the bike ride *you* want, you can bike with her to her trumpet lesson.

## GET IN THE GAME!
## ACT, ADJUST, ACT, ADJUST . . .

Now that you've completed your game plans and scorecards, it's time to start moving, bringing your ideas to the reality of your world. Begin to act on your plans. As you do, you'll find that you have to adjust your plans, and continue to do so, to keep making progress in the direction you've chosen.

Whenever you think it makes sense to do so, talk to the people who are affected by your experiments to find out from them how they see things. These conversations provide opportunities to garner support. If you've not yet done so, describe how you hope your plan will lead to meeting their expectations better. Listen carefully, so that you understand more about how their interests (as well as your own) are met through the actions you're initiating. And if it seems apt, explore with them other ways for how you might meet these expectations, either with further changes or with revisions to what you're now trying. Record notes on your insights from these conversations.

As you start taking action, begin filling in your scorecards. If you make any changes to your game plans or scorecards as a result of new information or ideas, then modify them accordingly.

Or let's say you set out to implement a new set of reporting relationships at work to help free you from mundane tasks that keep you from focusing on long-term planning for your business, while permitting you to be more available now for your family and your church. You might run up against the bureaucratic reality that certain jobs are graded in such a way that disallows the change in responsibilities you had in mind. So you substitute who will take on which tasks, without scuttling the innovation's overall thrust.

One of Victor's experiments included his plan to get up a bit earlier and do a twenty-minute workout every morning. He built in accountability pressure by making this known to his wife, but soon realized that it wasn't working; he failed to arise early. So he shifted gears: "I decided to adjust to exercising on either my bike or my elliptical machine for thirty minutes, four times a week, no matter what the time of day. Now it's working."

Roxanne's experiment to spend more time with her daughter, Cecile, was so successful that she had to rethink her own expectations—another kind of adjustment—about how available she could be, because Cecile just kept asking for more.

You already know that when you design your experiments, you are compelled to think about how a given innovation—be it having lunch with your buddies, working out with your wife, exploring a new business possibility, or altering the decision-making process in your work team—will affect stakeholders in all your domains to produce a four-way win. You probably solicited their input and support for your experiments in your dialogues, and on your scorecard you identified intended benefits for all domains, even if some of those benefits won't be seen for a while. Thinking about it this way encourages you to make adjustments to align your plans with what matters to others before you even start. Now that you're doing it, however, you're seeing things from a new point of view, so it's useful to check in with them and adjust, again.

The only thing you can count on is that you'll have to make adjustments. In fact, you'll need to be adjusting *continually*. That's a good thing. It's central to what I mean by being innovative as a leader in your life—acting with creativity by experimenting with how to get things done. Being able to shift in light of new information and in light of new opportunities is a skill. Practicing will make you a more confident leader of change, now and in the future.

One of Lim's experiments was to train for the Chicago Marathon with his boss, just after having his first child.

Describing to my stakeholders how this was going to positively impact them was critical in making it a success. Once I started training, my wife, Joanna, expressed more concerns about it than she had initially. She had said that having our first child should be an inspiration to continue our family's Chicago Marathon tradition, not a hurdle to prevent it. Now that we were just weeks away from the birth, however, the implications were weighing heavier. Those precious moments were the last we'd have alone for a while—two decades before we'd ship our child off to college!

She wondered aloud whether this was really the best time to be training for a marathon. How was I going to do 15- to 20-mile training runs when we were going to be getting up in the middle of the night to care for our baby? Joanna worried that my training runs would become less frequent and that I'd end up hurting my legs. In talking with her, though, I inadvertently uncovered major concerns from her, my stakeholder number one. I consulted my Total Leadership coaches for help, and one asked whether my wife's real concern was that I'd be too caught up in training during the first months of our baby's life to be as present a husband and father as she'd like. I hadn't honestly thought this through. And while my wife's fear of my possible injury was genuine, her big concern was that she just didn't see the marathon as a priority now.

This led me to see the importance of demonstrating small wins to Joanna. I needed to break the project into bite-sized tasks that I could quickly complete, and to show her that a game plan, metrics, and milestones were in place. It was critical for her to see progress and how she would share the benefits.

By talking to his wife as his experiment was unfolding, Lim became aware of what he needed to do to ensure her continued support. And there were ups and downs at work, too, that affected his plans, requiring adjustments.

The more that I ran, the more energized I was. Within six weeks of training, I lost six pounds and was incredibly focused at work. But my boss developed shin splints and had to back off of his training for a while. I spoke with him and asked how I could better support him. I assured him that I would understand if he wanted to cancel running the marathon. He appreciated my concern, which he admitted he had never experienced from his other direct reports! Thankfully, he was up and about before long.

Letting others in on his experiment, being relentlessly curious, and seeking to benefit others led Lim to unexpected gains, as he recounted two years later:

For my direct reports and Wharton pals, running together and talking about my experiment was invigorating. Word spread around campus, and everywhere I went, I'd get amazing questions about the marathon. I made strong friendships that continue to this day as a result of those runs.

At work, the runs gave me an opportunity to build trust and hear what people at work liked best and feared most about their careers in the company. One young team member had an idea about starting a college recruiting program for us and wondered whether I would support it and let him steer it. I applauded him for it. As we all enriched our relationships outside of the office, everyone saw that it was safe to bring ideas to me and volunteer openly for things. My boss and fellow partners saw that morale, profitability, and overall performance on my team were higher than in any other sector of our business, and that innovations like running with my staff contributed to these results.

Ultimately, I was well prepared for the marathon, because my wife was supportive through the training period. Joanna—who had only intended to be a spectator—met me at mile 13, and seeing me a little off pace, jumped in with no preparation (she's already a phenomenal athlete); and though she was only four months away from the birth, she ran the race all the way to the end with me!

Though my boss and I have now moved on to other companies, our friendship was cemented for life through this experience.

Like a good experimenter—a scientist, really—Lim had data that he was collecting along the way. He used new information as he gathered it, taking advantage of opportunities and gaining support as he progressed with his plan.

It is difficult to adjust experiments through simple intuition. Metrics allowed me to see when I was falling off pace on my training, or when we had a dip in our revenue month-to-month during the training period, or when there were fewer e-mails going back and forth with my boss regarding the marathon. Charting how often my wife and I were going to the gym each week was very telling. It pointed to how we had to recommit to our exercise regimen.

Lim's example shows that to change your world, you have to pay attention to what's happening around you as you're taking each new step in the direction you've chosen, and adjust. You have to try to make winners of those you care about.

## The Leadership Leap

You take what I call the *leadership leap* when you jump into *their* hearts and minds. Len Schlesinger, currently vice chairman and COO of Limited Brands, put this in a direct and profoundly simple way when he spoke to one of my Wharton classes recently: "It's not about you. The sooner you learn this lesson, the better off you'll be."

It's so easy to get caught up in your own ideas about the way the world should work, and miss the opportunity to focus on what others need from you. But the real world is one of interdependent people, and you have to find a way to connect your ideas with the needs of the people upon whom you depend to get important things done. And when you do this—when you take the time to discover how your interests are aligned with those of others and then adapt accordingly—you are much more likely to realize your aspirations.

Leaders see the world through the eyes of others, as you did in your stakeholder dialogues. They aim to make the world better for the people around them, as you are now doing in your experiments. In what might seem paradoxical, the more you take self-interest out of the picture and instead *do for others*, the more you end up benefiting your own interests, in both the short and the long term.

Leaders see "we" where others see only "me." That conception of "we" can go beyond those most intimate and dear, and thus can inspire great achievement. Bono, U2's lead singer and a global advocate for social change, is a rock star, of course, yet much of his music and the full body of the rest of his work is about making things better for people in need. Indra Nooyi, PepsiCo's CEO, is now pursuing "performance with purpose."[1] She wants to make money, of course, but in a way that serves the world's need for healthy foods; this will, in turn, she hopes, enrich all.

That leaders succeed when they do for others is something most Total Leadership participants realize more clearly from their stakeholder assessments and dialogues. And when you design and—especially—implement your experiments, it becomes clearer still. The best experiments are those that don't just get approval from all your key stakeholders, but will genuinely benefit them by changing their worlds for the better. You demonstrate leadership by choosing to do something other people care about as much as, if not more than, you do. And this increases the chances of your success.

Consider an experiment in which you set out to work from home one day a week. How much more likely to succeed will it be if your boss plays a direct role in holding you accountable for actually staying home—and is rooting for you? For your boss, the arrangement in a well-designed experiment should be as good as, or even better than, it is for you! To make this happen requires that you've got to believe that it *will* be good for him, as well as for your other key stakeholders. If you can't convince yourself that this really is true, then you're not going to be very persuasive.

In one of his experiments, Victor took a big step toward overcoming inhibitions holding him back from trying something new.

The goal was to extend my role at work from general and project management to include working with groups outside my area on some systems we were building. Someone had to start defining the business direction for these systems, and I wanted to challenge myself, to get out of my comfort zone and feel more fulfilled at work. I expected that would positively affect my other domains.

I had to explain the rationale, and in a series of discussions with my boss, peers, and others, I got their buy-in. I also had to make a public commitment to my new role. I had to make sure I was proposing something that wasn't just for me. I laid the groundwork by delegating some of my current responsibilities to my team members. I found ways to give them more opportunities to contribute to our group's customer service goals. Delegating built morale all around; people feel more involved.

My boss came to see not only that he and the other people he manages would benefit from having someone define the business direction for our new systems, but that it would be good for them if I stretched myself at work. There was a payoff all around. In effect, my experiment became his experiment and that of my coworkers.

When you actually believe you're doing for others, you don't feel guilty about doing something that might seem as if it's just for you. In *Work and Family—Allies or Enemies?* Jeff Greenhaus and I observed that more time spent by mothers on themselves results in better emotional health in their kids.[2] This means going to the spa without guilt because you know you're doing something positive for your children, too. To do for others, you *do* need to care for yourself—and your experiments should reflect that truth and be rooted in what you earlier wrote about being real.

With your experiments, you're taking the opportunity to try new ways of getting things done to get closer to your leadership vision, and you are also enhancing your ability to perform and to feel satisfied about your performance, in all domains. Your success hinges on your ability to win support, on believing that your goal is to make things better for all your stakeholders. What you're trying to achieve is about something bigger than yourself—a higher purpose.

## Be Artfully Political

It's useful to operate from a political point of view—that is, to act in the interests of the collective and to help others to see how the interests of others are served by any initiative. As President Dwight Eisenhower famously said, "Leadership is the art of getting someone else to do something you want done because he wants to do it." Operating in the interests of the collective (whether it's your family, company, or social club) increases your influence and impact in a group or organization. Yet many people see politics as mere manipulation. But as Joel DeLuca observes in his book *Political Savvy*, politically smart individuals don't manipulate out of self-interest. They care a lot about ideas that can benefit others and their organizations. They don't flinch in the face of political barriers, but seek to overcome them by creating something new that takes into account and serves the agendas of those around them. What he calls "enlightened self-interest" is another way to describe the spirit of four-way wins.[3]

DeLuca explains how the conventional view of politics blocks us from taking action to produce positive change. Too many people are unwilling to advocate for their ideas, lest they be seen as pushing for something for themselves. That's the "moral block": you feel that it's just wrong to "manipulate" other people. In other cases, you forsake opportunities to lead because you don't realize the importance of actively working to get others on your side. This "rational block" gets in the way when you believe your idea is a great one, and if other people don't see it the same way, you can just forget about them. Both blocks to taking initiative must be overcome.

Manipulation occurs only if what you're up to serves your interests and not the collective interests. And in the end, if you don't align your interests with those of others, you're not going to create that critical mass of support you need to further your interests.

Victor demonstrated his understanding of this lesson:

As I've implemented my experiments, I've met some resistance and even confronted some apathy. I've learned that if I keep in mind that what I'm doing serves not just me but also my stakeholders, I can communicate my plan in a way that gains their support.

I was astounded by the positive effect we had at work when my colead and I spent time just talking to people about the system we're building and listened to their perspective on how it can help them.

Victor, by believing in his goals and by talking about the interests he was pursuing, kept his agenda open, not hidden. This instilled trust and got a responsive hearing. Yet by simply talking about what he was aiming to accomplish, Victor affected real change, for he became more aware of himself as a leader. As DeLuca's research shows, politically savvy people

BRING OTHERS ALONG WITH YOU 161

know that making mistakes is not failure; the only real failure, they believe, is the failure to try to make an impact. Just taking the initiative to make a difference, in other words, is ennobling, even if your experiment ultimately fails. You see yourself differently, as do others, when you take action to change your world.

Think about the leader you wrote about in chapter 2. I'll bet that some of what you admire about this person is what he or she did to make the world better somehow, fulfilling what you might see as a spiritual purpose with his or her life, even in what might be a very small way. A leader has to care about making a difference, about doing for others. Leaders improve the world in a way that fits with their vision of the kind of person they want to become and the kind of world they want to live in. Was your admired leader acting manipulatively or, rather, acting to build support and influence others in the interests of the collective?

## SERVE *THEIR* INTERESTS

This exercise, which you can do at any point during your experiments, extends the previous exercise by focusing on your reactions to the impact of your experiments.

Take a few moments to think about how to improve your chances of success by again considering what's in it for *them*, the people affected by the changes you're now making. Also, how do you feel about serving their interests?

Consider these issues and discuss them with your coaches or any trusted advisers:

- First, identify the specific ways in which each person or group affected by the changes you're making is benefiting from what you're doing. Then write a sentence or two about how you feel about making these contributions.

- If you feel proud of what you're doing, list the reasons and brainstorm ideas for what it would take to enhance these feelings. If you draw a blank, then think about what information you need to be able to generate such ideas and how you might get that information, and from whom.

- If you feel guilt or fear about what you're doing, list the reasons and then brainstorm ideas for what it would take to minimize these feelings. If you draw a blank, then think about what information you need to be able to generate such ideas and how you might get that information, and from whom.

On the basis of what you know now, what other ideas do you have for what it would take to enhance your confidence as a leader who creates meaningful change?

Another thing about politically savvy people is that they are more likely to give credit than take it. They share success, letting others show their competence and helping to build the confidence of people around them. They make winners out of their partners. This enhances their reputation as people committed to helping others and makes it more likely that others will see them as trustworthy, as someone others are willing, even eager, to help. It's a good idea to find opportunities to acknowledge publicly the contributions others make to anything new you're trying to get done.

## Induce Reciprocity

We've established how when you're leading change, it's useful to take a small-wins approach and to ensure that others see your experiment as theirs. But to produce four-way wins throughout your life, you need to cultivate a supportive network of relationships in all domains.

You do this by ensuring that your experiments enhance the strength of these relationships. It is a virtuous cycle you can instigate and then accelerate as you get better and better through practice: contribute to others now to create more support for your capacity to contribute in the future.

One way to contribute to the success of others is by building connections with and among people. This is the law of reciprocity, the engine of social capital, which is the store of the resources available to you through and in your networks of relationships in your life. "These resources include information, ideas, leads, opportunities, financial capital, power, emotional support, even goodwill, trust, and cooperation," explains Wayne Baker in *Achieving Success Through Social Capital*.[4]

Successful leaders consciously cultivate networks that enable them to achieve their goals, fulfill their missions, realize their visions, and make their contributions to the world. Nearly all Total Leadership participants report that their stakeholder dialogues and the engagement of others in their experiments build stronger connections within an enriched web of relationships. This happens because the emphasis is on making life better for others. When you take this as your purpose, the law of reciprocity is likely to kick in.

Reciprocity is a universal concept, an essential attribute of human relationships, which contains this paradox: it is by giving that you get. You invoke reciprocity's power when you help others without expecting immediate returns. Most of the world's religions teach that it's better to give than to receive. Yet for many of us, it's actually harder to receive than to give. In an exercise on social capital in my classes, each person asks for help on something, and all, then, offer support that's either direct ("Here's how I'll help you") or indirect ("I'll introduce you to someone who can help you").[5] Almost everyone enjoys the giving part but finds the asking part uncomfortable. And it's not only because they feel giving is better for them because it induces reciprocity; it also makes most people feel good. Such acts build our connection to others and enhance our feeling of belonging.

Again, the most effective approach for building a strong network is to see the purpose of doing so as contributing to the success of others, not taking from them. This is the ideology that John F. Kennedy declared in one of the defining speeches of his generation: "Ask not what your country can do for you. Ask what you can do for your country." Your experiments are opportunities for you to contribute to others and thus induce long-term reciprocity.

## Connect Others, Make Your World Smaller

We humans tend to build networks that are closed—that is, made up of people who are like us, who know each other. We tend to be clannish and feel most comfortable with people who look and behave as we do. Yet you'll gain the greatest benefit by adopting an open approach to network building—connecting to people and groups who don't know each other—even if this requires you to stretch beyond your normal social circles. Research shows that you obtain the greatest access to the resources available to you through networks when you expand your range of contacts. Don't worry so much about how many there are; focus instead on the variety of groups you inhabit. And don't fake it: join with others who are pursuing goals that have real meaning to you.

Social capital is a portable, lifelong asset that compounds over time, so it's wise to have an investment strategy for developing yours. Look for ways of connecting people, and make your world smaller: connecting people reaps benefits all around, which is why open networks trump closed ones. When you're in the midst of an open network, you can fill what network researchers call "structural holes." Let's say you know

John and Mary, but John and Mary don't know each other. You believe that connecting them would be to their mutual benefit. Introduce them, and you've filled a structural hole in your network.

John and Mary might begin to collaborate on a project or strike up a friendship. How would you feel about that result? Probably pretty good, for you've made the world a bit more connected. But more important, how would they feel? Most likely they'd feel good, too. They'd be grateful to you, and they'd credit you for bringing them together. You've filled the structural hole by being a bridge, connecting people who should be connected but weren't. You've capitalized on a latent opportunity in your world; because you've tried to help, the law of reciprocity is likely to work down the road.

Of course, there's no reason to be limited to people within a particular domain. Opportunities for you to connect people from different domains abound, and you're likely to find them just by looking. Indeed, one of the benefits of the Total Leadership program is that because you're focused on how all your domains fit and benefit each other, you're much more likely to see opportunities for linking people in the different parts of your life.

## IDENTIFY THE MISSING PIECES IN YOUR NETWORK

To realize the full support your networks can provide for being a better leader and having a richer life, it's a good idea to first identify the groups on which you depend.

You've already identified your key stakeholders, your immediate and intimate circle. For a quick audit of your current network and what you need to do to cultivate it, think about and write notes on these questions:

- Which ties should you strengthen, and where should you spend less time and energy?

- Which networks can help you in particular ways?

- Who can help you develop skills and competencies you need to progress?

- Who might provide valuable political and personal counsel?

- Who are the people who influence others on topics that are meaningful to you?

## The Trust Market

If you don't have people who trust you, then you cannot be a leader who gets things done with and through others. The more you're seen as doing for others, the more trustworthy you will be to those who know you, and, indirectly, the more you will be known as trustworthy among the many people who know the people you know. Your reputation ripples rapidly out into the wider world.

To cultivate social capital is to enhance your value in the marketplace for trust. That is, your reputation will be better as the belief in your trustworthiness increases among those who see you pursuing the interests of others. People are more likely to feel good about you and to support you if you share credit for achievements and aim first to give, not get. You grow your reputation as someone trustworthy as you create value for others and connect them.

One means for cultivating trust by contributing to others is by delegating tasks to them, by helping them to grow. Jenna heard people at work bluntly ask her why she didn't delegate to them instead of "wasting her time" doing things she didn't need to be doing. She figured out that she needed to experiment with giving her team members greater autonomy, so she could concentrate more on strategy while enhancing the trust her team had in her. Similarly, Ismail realized that "a good goal would be to work on having more trust in people around me." He altered the decision-making structure of his company and put power into the hands of people for whom he had typically made decisions. And in doing so he's begun to build a stronger, more trusting leadership team while freeing up time for other important things in his life.

## Make a Difference, Beyond What You Can See

If there's one thing that's consistent in every great leader, it's that they inspire others with their passionate commitment to what they believe in. They love what they're doing and they're doing what they love. People want to share not only in their success but also in that passion. Where does it come from and how do they bring it to life? It comes from their integrity—the desire to contribute, to make connections, and to increase the sense that people belong to something bigger. And it comes from their authenticity—the commitment to act with purpose.

Indeed, it's hard to see how someone without a genuine sense of purpose can really be a leader at all. The commitment of leaders to their cause not only inspires others, but also gives them the courage to try and the will to keep going when they meet obstacles. When you're true to yourself, act according to your values, respect and do for others, and creatively implement change to benefit those around you, then you are more likely to foster the meaningful connections with your stakeholders that are a hallmark of great leaders.

Just thinking more about the impact of your everyday actions on stakeholders beyond your inner circle can make the world a better place. There are countless simple ways you can do this. In designing your experiments, you had to give some consideration to your community domain.

Even the small indirect ways in which your experiments positively affect your community can be important in how you see yourself as a leader.

Take a closer look at your community domain. You might do nothing more than simply (and yet profoundly) thinking about how your work and career do—or how they might better—contribute to improving the world around you. But it might mean more than this. You might begin to focus more actively on the social responsibility of your business. Or on perhaps a smaller scale, you might reconsider your role as a parent: how more focused attention to raising your children well while you go about the business of producing economic gain results in a contribution to the greater good.

Keep in mind your role in the world beyond your family, your work relationships, and your immediate social network as you progress with your experiments. Of course, you don't have to construe it in any specific way or adopt any particular set of values about community, or any other aspect of life. Investing in your community might mean joining a local board, caring for neighbors and friends, giving time to environmental causes, participating in religious or political groups, or giving money to charities that help the less fortunate. It might also mean reckoning the work you do to make money in light of its ultimate social impact. The more you focus on community in your experiments, the more likely it is that you'll enhance your sense of meaningful purpose and feel inspired to see the experiment through.

## GROW YOUR NETWORK

Your experiments have the potential to enrich your networks and the support that's in them. This in turn will strengthen your motivation for pursuing your experiments. Think about and write a few sentences in response to these questions:

- How will you share credit for the success of your experiments?

- How might your experiments provide opportunities to expand your range of contacts?

- How might you bring together people from different domains for mutual gain?

- How might your experiments fill structural holes and make the world smaller?

- How might your experiments give you opportunities to contribute and feel a greater sense of belonging to something beyond your circle of work, family, and friends?

## Gaining Strength to Keep Moving Your Ideas Forward

In Total Leadership experiments, people confront common obstacles to change: fear, guilt, and ignorance. You gain support for your innovations by adjusting as needed to ensure that all parties come out as winners. You engage your stakeholders in your experiments and make headway toward achieving greater performance and satisfaction in all your life domains. You realize your successes because, first, you thought about how to best align your actions and values (looking from the inside out), and, second, you considered how to contribute to others' success as a way of building trust and support (looking from the outside in).

People want to feel that the parts of their lives fit together well, in a way that makes sense to them. And they want to feel that they belong and are contributing to interests beyond their immediate circle. Stakeholder analyses bring to light how the people and interests in the different parts of our lives are interconnected, a microcosm of the larger social world. For many, a shift in awareness—from your small part of the world to the world beyond your everyday purview—follows naturally from thinking about the community as a stakeholder and analyzing the relationships among all your stakeholders. It isn't much of a stretch to envision how your inner circle fans out to touch many others indirectly. The more you can keep this in mind, the stronger your resolve is likely to be as you hit bumps on the road with your experiments.

When you're trying to make something new happen, you've got to know what other people care about, so that you can adjust your actions. And you've got to know whom they trust, so that you know who will listen to whom as you seek to exert influence. With this knowledge, you can move innovative ideas faster and with less resistance, directing these ideas through people who trust each other.

As you become known as someone who contributes to others' successes, and as you are seen as a trustworthy person in your different worlds, you will have greater access to one of the most important benefits of social capital: you'll know who trusts whom. In turn, you're more likely to succeed, to find the smartest path to gaining support for your ideas to make things better and better.

## CHAPTER 8

# Conclusion

## *Reflect and Grow*

TOTAL LEADERSHIP doesn't end with the implementation of your experiments. This is really just the beginning. Being a better leader and having a richer life is an ongoing search, which I hope you will be on for the rest of your life. As long as you continue practicing authenticity, integrity, and creativity, you will increase your chances of scoring four-way wins—performing better and finding satisfaction in your various domains.

Becoming a better leader requires constant reflection—making sense of your experience and then discovering ways to use your insights to increase your impact. Then, to stay ever sharp, it's good to teach what you've learned (and then try to teach what you still *want* to learn). Learning leadership by doing it—what's called *action learning*, which is what you've been engaged in through your efforts with this book—is effective only when you take the time to reflect on what worked, what didn't work, and what you might do differently in the future. Looking back is a necessary step in the process of learning and performance improvement in which you've invested much so far. If you give short shrift to the task of reflection, then the lessons don't get internalized. They don't last.

Looking back, Lim, an optimist by temperament, saw each of his experiments as an adventure, and he realized how important it was to have utter faith in what he was doing.

It's clear to me now that you really have to believe in your experiments. I believe in mine; they truly reflect my life and my values. I see no option other than to try my best to succeed with them. I convey this zeal when I talk to people and they see it in my actions. Innovating in ways that help you express your true passion helps to sustain momentum through hard times.

Other people sense when you have passion for what you're pursuing, and they are inclined to be inspired, too. Passionate commitment gives you the will to persist in finding ways to get around the obstacles that are always in the way of something new. Lim came to realize this more clearly—it really hit home—when he reflected on his experiments and what they taught him about leadership in his life. This is what you'll be doing in this final chapter.

This last part is about what's transpired since you started this book and what it means for your future. It's a chance not only to check your experiments specifically against your scorecards—to see the extent to which you did, after all, achieve the four-way wins you aimed for—but more generally, and more importantly, to articulate what you've learned about yourself, your stakeholders, and being a leader intent on living a richer life. This last chapter prepares you to build further support for your leadership vision and to tell your leadership story as a way of transmitting what you've learned to others.

Six to eight weeks after having begun your experiments is an ideal time for you to take stock and reflect. By now you've designed experiments and implemented them. You've traveled some distance in a new direction. You may have been working with colleagues or friends as coaches, or shared your journey so far with others at www.totalleadership.org. Now you'll take a fresh look at what you've done.

Measuring your progress is a momentum enhancer. Writing responses to the questions I ask at this stage might feel like a bit of a pain, but I'm certain it will be worth the new insights and energy you'll gain about what you've accomplished and about who you are—and who you want to be—as a leader in all parts of your life.

Let's scroll back, then, in reverse order, starting with the results of your experiments, then to your analysis of changes in performance in meeting stakeholder expectations, then to where things stand now with your satisfaction with and alignment among domains, and finally to your baseline—to see how you've progressed toward the goals you wanted to pursue when you first began this book. After distilling the main lessons you've learned, you'll take a look at how, through the systematic pursuit of four-way wins, you've grown as a leader, now more practiced at acting with authenticity, integrity, and creativity, and what your plans are for continuing your development as a leader in the future.

## Revisiting Your Goals and Metrics

When you designed your experiments, you developed goals in each domain for every experiment along with metrics for both results and actions, customized for your particular experiments. Action metrics, as you recall, allow you to track the progress of your behavior (e.g., the number of times you do something), and results metrics give you proof that you have achieved your goals—or not.

Ismail did three experiments. The first was to restructure his company and his role in it. He saw this "as a way to create an opportunity I

> ## REVIEW YOUR SCORECARDS
>
> Review the scorecards you produced in chapter 6. In whatever way is most convenient for you, describe the data you gathered from all sources for the metrics—both actions and results—you developed for your experiments.
>
> Note any other changes you've observed in performance in any domain, or in the relationship among different domains. And explain how and why your goals, metrics, results, and time frame might have changed as a consequence of new information or unexpected situations that arose.

had come to realize I needed, to build stronger connections with the other parts of my life and the people who matter. I needed time and psychic energy to make that happen." His first experiment created firmer boundaries among different domains and allowed for more focused attention in all of them.

For his second experiment, Ismail spent prescheduled time with his children every Friday. He would pick them up from school and spend the afternoon and evening doing things together. He needed his three business partners and all of his direct reports to allow him that time, permission for which he got by talking it over with them. The feelings he now has about his relationships with his sons have spilled over into the rest of his life, and he reflected this in his updated four circles graphic, with more overlap of his family and other circles.

His third experiment was to equip executives in his company with smart phones, to make it possible to resolve customer issues and make business decisions without having to be at the office. The experiment increased productivity through better use of time, reduced the need for face-to-face communication, and eliminated waste associated with having to set up laptops at remote locations to discuss and make decisions on tactical matters. "It made me available to deal with work issues at all times," Ismail later told me, "while I could be physically where it mattered most."

He was systematic in gathering data to verify and quantify the results of his experiments. He used Microsoft Outlook to track scheduled activities and the specific scores he gave along the way. "Friday evenings," he said, "became major milestones, as much of the data had to be gathered on Friday and recorded." He also developed spreadsheets to use as scoring tools to measure his progress on a continual basis in each of the important areas he had designated.

There is no one best way to gather and track data. Whatever way works best for you is the way to go. Ismail captured his results metrics in a chart that had two rows for each domain (one for each of the two measures per domain), a column for describing these measures he was assessing, and then six more columns to record his rating (using a 1–10 scale) each week on each of the measures. In the final column, for each metric he calculated the percentage of change compared with his initial rating, and this allowed him to see, at the end of a six-week period, the progress he'd made over his baseline. Ismail tracked his action metrics during the span of his experiments using a similar method.

Roxanne took a different approach.

For my first experiment, metrics were clustered around several objectives: reduce my stress level so that I could appropriately engage in the activity at hand; increase my involvement in the activity by reducing distractions and the need to focus inward; and strengthen my connection to my children and their lives. For the first two of these, I gathered much of my data by using my "gut feelings" as a barometer versus using independent, objective metrics. I documented my stress level on a 1–10 scale at the end of each workday, when it tends to be highest. I also kept track of the number of times I needed to remind myself to refocus during the week, and I gathered input from my children about how they enjoyed our activities. Plus, I kept track of how many new pieces of personal information about my children's lives I learned as we engaged in the activity.

In another example, Sally Garcia, a Total Leadership participant who directs plant operations at a large manufacturing firm, designed an experiment to enhance her staff's ability to monitor some of its functions by integrating new technology into everyday operations. This reduced the amount of time spent to determine the status of department subunits from twelve hours per week to only one, eliminated much of the arduous physical activity associated with the previous data processing system, and made it possible to view data in real time from any computer in or outside of the plant, enhancing the soundness of managers' business decisions.

She also set specific financial metrics, and they were met over the course of the experiment: cost reductions of some $125,000, cost avoidance topping $15,000, and productivity increases translating into about $25,000. Customer relations improved because department personnel could react sooner to quality and maintenance concerns. Plus, because as manager she didn't have to keep such close tabs on everything, she found herself able to focus on a new round of improvements. These business results coincided with changes in the lives of people at the plant. "We all have time and mental energy to focus on other things that matter: coaching softball, working with the Boy Scouts, helping out at Special Olympics, fund-raising for the Juvenile Diabetes Association," Sally reported. "I can see how the people in my department bring back to work each day the fulfillment they feel from the meaningful things they can do outside work, and it strengthens our resolve to work smarter and better."

These are three illustrations of the many different ways to document your progress, in experiments that worked well. Some metrics, of course, will register failure to achieve desired results. Innovation comes at the risk of potential failure. Keep in mind that the benefits of the Total Leadership approach come from experimenting, and not just from meeting specific targets. The only real failures are the failure to try to make an impact or the failure to learn something from your effort that can propel you forward, as André explained in describing what he learned from one of his experiments—systematically increasing and refining his contact database—that had mixed results:

> I realized that I just wasn't sufficiently motivated. This lack of motivation, I believe, is because expanding my database of contacts was too far removed from actually doing something for others. Initiating change must always involve those around me—something I succeeded in doing with my other experiments. Because I didn't feel accountable to anyone in this aspect of my experiment, I never really made it a priority. The fundamental differences I see between where I succeeded and failed in my experiments was the direct emphasis on making others happy, of doing for others, as a motivator for my actions.

Your own metrics may point to success or failure. André's pointed in both directions. Like most, he used his experience to learn an important leadership lesson despite the fact that one of his experiments did not produce the four-way win he was after.

## Revisiting Stakeholder Expectations

Let's turn to where things now stand with your stakeholders. Earlier you described and assessed performance expectations of your stakeholders and theirs of you. Now is a good time to reevaluate. In chapter 4, you prepared a chart that laid out those expectations. You rated, on a scale of 1 to 10, how you were doing and how they were doing. How do you rate performance in meeting these expectations now?

## REVIEW STAKEHOLDER EXPECTATIONS

Go to chapter 4 and read your stakeholder expectations charts. Reevaluate your ratings of performance in meeting expectations, and in a convenient place, perhaps on the original chart or on a new one (whatever works for you), record the scores as of now.

What changes do you observe, and how do you account for them? And to what extent did changes in one (or more) domains affect changes in other domains?

Most Total Leadership participants find that being real, being whole, and being innovative—by sharing their values and visions with stakeholders, winning their support for experiments, and creatively serving their interests—pays real dividends in meeting, or exceeding, expectations. On average, participants rate their performance in meeting the expectations of their key stakeholders in the work domain as 7.2 out of 10 at the start of their Total Leadership experience and 7.8 at the end, about three months later—about a 9 percent gain, as I reported in chapter 1. The greatest gains, though, are in the self and family domains, at 25 percent and 15 percent, respectively. These gains are accompanied by gains in the community domain as well, of 12 percent. Improved performance in all domains—or, in other words, four-way wins.

Roxanne created a then-and-now chart to compare her stakeholder performance ratings. Here's how she described the changes she observed in almost every stakeholder relationship.

When I initially did these ratings, I made some inaccurate appraisals of what people expected of me, particularly at home. I felt I was constantly making sacrifices at the expense of my self and family to be able to contribute more fully at work. But I discovered from my stakeholders that my expectations were unrealistic, that I was being overly critical of myself in the work domain, and that I wasn't as aware as I needed to be of my children's needs. The big difference is that now I'm feeling much better, having clarified—and in some cases changed—these expectations. With my experiments, I've learned to make more conscious choices about how to meet them.

Intentional change by leaders trying to make things better in all four domains, to have richer lives—that's what the Total Leadership program is about. It's important to assess how you've improved performance in one domain while improving performance in other domains, either directly or indirectly. Kerry, the pharmaceutical marketing executive from San Francisco, shows how, when you're looking for it, you're more likely to find synergy—positive connections that are mutually enriching—across domains, even if unexpectedly.

One of my experiments was to do volunteer work and so directly improve performance and satisfaction in my self and community domains and, indirectly, the others. While I had some ideas about how this might affect my career, I really wasn't sure how this was going to play out. I got involved in helping organize our local Race for the Cure to raise awareness of breast cancer and money for research. Doing this has helped me feel more connected to a cause I care about.

But there was an unexpected bonus: I've also managed, through this experiment, to improve performance directly in my work domain. I encouraged my boss's wife to come to one of our meetings, and she and I have since become two of the most active organizers. My boss is thrilled. He gets to spend time with his son, his wife is happier because she's engaged in meaningful social action, and he's grateful and feels closer to me, even as I'm fulfilling goals I had for other parts of my life. Many lives enriched in many domains!

Kerry's innovation is just one example of how thinking creatively using an analysis of your stakeholders' interests can produce rewards all the way around. My hope is that by now you too are seeing, in new and realistic ways, how the relationship of work and the rest of your life need not be a zero-sum game—in which one part wins while the other loses—but, rather, how these connections are ripe with opportunities for mutual benefit.

## Revisiting the Four-Way View

Now let's go further back and reexamine what you said about what really matters to you, how satisfied you are with the different parts of your life, and what has changed.

### REVIEW WHAT'S IMPORTANT

Go to chapter 2. Read your leadership vision and core values exercises. What revisions might you make, if any, to your vision—the story of your future—as a result of what you've done since you first wrote it? Are there any changes in your values? Note your observations.

Now go back to chapter 3, and without writing anything in response to the follow-on questions, simply redo the four-way attention chart, redraw your four circles (you can do this as often as you like and then compare to earlier versions using the tool at www.totalleadership.org), and reassess your domain satisfaction. Again, write about what's changed and what's stayed the same.

Kerry, thought about whether her values had changed:

All of my core values—achievement and personal development, affiliation, balance, collaboration, family and friendship, loyalty, integrity, and wisdom—remain very important to me. The difference is that now I appreciate them even more, because I'm more true to them than ever. I think of this now as authenticity. Back when I first wrote them out, I wasn't living a life fully committed to these values. It feels now as if I'm on that path.

Like Kerry, Roxanne changed neither her values nor her vision as a result of going through the Total Leadership program. But she benefited from articulating what she really cares about and then designing experiments that would change her life accordingly.

In writing my leadership vision, I was particularly surprised about a couple of things related to work. I had long thought that I wanted to leave my current job right after getting my MBA, and perhaps become a consultant. It turns out that wasn't part of my vision. I realized that what I really want is a challenging career that allows me to deepen my relationship with my children and my husband.

If neither your vision nor your values have changed, this doesn't mean you haven't made progress. Some people revise what's important to them, while others don't alter a thing. What most participants say at this stage is that they are now more *aware* of what matters. As a result, they're more committed to acting in a way that's consistent with their values and their aspirations for the world they want to create.

My research on the changes that participants report on the four-way attention chart shows that the importance people attach to their different domains doesn't change much. What changes, instead, is the focus of their time and energy: less on work and more on other things. The good news is that this pattern coincides with increases in satisfaction in *all* domains, including work (up 21 percent), home (28 percent), community (31 percent), and self (39 percent). Even better, as we saw earlier, performance increases across the board, too.

When Victor completed his before-and-after analysis of the four-way attention chart and of his satisfaction ratings, he found that he had made positive gains in satisfaction in three of his four life domains (all but community) and for his life as a whole. He did so *without* having to make trade-offs. Victor found himself in a good position to build on these positive steps, to raise his satisfaction and performance levels even higher with further experiments.

When he looked at the alignment of his values and actions, he found what first appeared to be an incongruity in his updated four-way attention chart: an *increase* in the importance of work, coupled with a *decrease* in the time and energy he devotes in that domain.

> I've acknowledged that work is important to me at this stage in my life, and I've adjusted my ratings of work and family importance accordingly. I definitely view this as subject to change, and can imagine situations in which family switches around in its importance. But, meanwhile, I've succeeded in reducing the amount of time and energy I apply to work, mainly by virtue of delegating more as I clear the decks and prepare to extend my role into newer areas. I couldn't have done this without involving my stakeholders on my new leadership path.

Let's continue the then-and-now comparisons with your four circles, another tool for examining the alignment of what's important with what you do in the different parts of your life. Have your dialogues and experiments helped you get closer to the ideal of concentric circles—the rings inside a tree—instead of a lake dotted with distinct ripples from a scattershot of stones? Compare the circles you drew in chapter 3 and the ones you just drew now. What's different, and what does this tell you?

Victor's circles became more overlapping, though certainly not fully. Figure 8-1 shows what his looked like, before (left) and after (right).

FIGURE 8-1

**Victor's four circles, before and after**

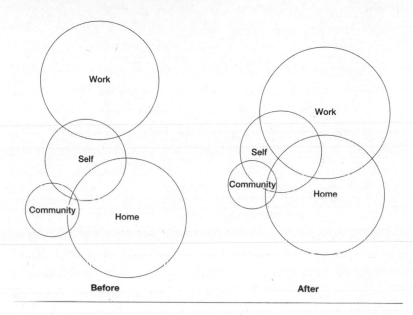

Before

After

When Lim redrew his circles a few months after drawing his first version, he noted that there was now greater overlap of the circles, but still not enough, which led him to think:

> One challenge is to incorporate my family and friends more into my life. I'm relocating in my new job to where I grew up, and it's where my parents, brother, and a whole community of close friends reside. I want to incorporate the lessons from my experiments further with this community. I have to take what I've learned and make it part of the corporate philosophy at my new company. I was hired, in part, for my ability to make things happen.

If I follow through on my plan of action and stay true to my leadership vision, my circles will continue to overlap more and more over time. I'll focus in particular on staying open-minded and experimenting, trying not to get too rigid in my thinking.

It's useful to consider what you did that led to more or less overlap in your four circles. This helps you to see what you learned so far and gives you ideas about things you can do to achieve greater and greater overlap in the future.

## Return to Your Baseline

Now let's go back to the very start. In the first exercise of this book, you established a baseline, noting your initial goals for reading this book. Let's review the progress you've made toward these goals.

This will help you understand better what you've accomplished, and it will help you identify what's next on your journey toward becoming the leader you really want to be. Everyone who reads this book has learned different things. The important point for you is to be sure you record, in whatever way will be most memorable to you, the lessons that you want to hold on to so that you can remember and use them in the future.

---

### RETURN TO YOUR BASELINE

Go back to the very first exercise (your goals for the Total Leadership program). Read what you wrote about your goals. Did your goals change since you wrote them? Write notes on whether you achieved them and why you did or did not.

## Leadership Lessons

Now that you've invested the time in looking back and seeing what you've done since you began, boil it down to the essential takeaways.

---

### DISTILL YOUR LEADERSHIP LESSONS

To capture your main lessons learned, write a paragraph or so on these three questions:

- What is the most important thing you've learned about being the leader you want to be?

- How does acting with authenticity (being real), integrity (being whole), and creativity (being innovative) affect your ability to score four-way wins?

- What have you learned about meeting the performance expectations of key stakeholders?

---

"Strangely enough, I felt like a fulfilling personal life was a luxury I could not afford, given my career ambitions," Roxanne said. "I don't feel that way now." Viewing herself as a leader in all parts of her life, getting smarter and more creative about how she could experiment with new ways of getting things done that worked for her, her work, and the rest of her life, changed her aspirations. André came to a different realization:

As I've worked on my leadership skills, I've discovered that much of the misalignment that I originally felt existed between me and my stakeholders was because of misunderstandings, invalid assumptions, or poor communication. This existed especially with my sister: I felt I was underperforming in certain areas, while she saw me as overperforming. To her, I had taken on too much responsibility. I heard this consistently in my dialogues, and now I've been able to achieve far greater agreement on expectations. All it took was a simple recognition that I wasn't doing as badly as I thought.

I see now that you cannot accurately assess your life and what you need to do to make changes until you understand the state of affairs with your stakeholders. What do they need and expect from you, and what do you need and expect from them? It's an absolute imperative aspect of setting and achieving goals—but I just hadn't realized it before. You don't know where and how far you need to go if you do not have this understanding.

And here's what Lim said about what he learned about being a leader:

One of the really great lessons I continue to build on is that when you take risks, you need to let your stakeholders know that you're making yourself vulnerable. Ask for their help as you innovate, and they'll invariably step up to the plate; they become the stakeholders you "expect" them to be. I see more clearly now that describing to stakeholders why what I do is important to me, and how it will have a positive impact on them, is a powerful ally in getting things done. It gives me courage.

There's always some risk when you try new things. Effective leaders, though, at all levels in organizations and in different stages of life, muster the courage to persist by working to identify and minimize resistance, from inside and out, and by realizing how their initiatives serve purposes beyond what they can sniff with their own noses. They never stop searching for new ways to contribute their talent and energy to causes they believe in. They inspire others to focus energy on the collective good; by doing so, they inspire others to experiment.

They continue learning their whole lives. And they encourage people to learn from their experiences, from trial and error, knowing that this builds strength as well as the resilience to take on new challenges. Now that you've systematically reviewed your progress and distilled the main lessons you've learned, let's conclude by looking at the ways in which you are a better leader and what's next on your journey toward a richer life.

## What's Different as a Result of Your Practicing Authenticity, Integrity, and Creativity?

Leadership is a performing art. Your instrument is you. Like great musicians and great athletes, you will get better if you see yourself as a developing leader, watch other leaders, practice, and remain open to good coaching.

You have embarked on a journey to make yourself into a better leader and to have a richer, more integrated life as you've pursued four-way wins. Your continued success will come as you put what you've learned into lifelong practice. Your experiments to this point are only the beginning. Total Leadership is not a one-time fix. And this challenge of learning leadership and integrating the different parts of life isn't easy. Indeed, it's hard. There are limits and obstacles to surmount at every turn. With only twenty-four hours in the day, you just can't do it all.

Yet you've begun to change how you see yourself as a leader, as did Jenna, André, Kerry, Victor, Roxanne, Lim, Ismail, and the others you've read about. You picked up this book, wanting to transform something, and my hope is that today, through the force of your own actions, you feel more grounded, connected, and excited about the future.

You have chosen to be a different kind of leader, one who consciously tries to make things better in the real world, today, by being real, being whole, and being innovative. In chapter 1, figure 1-1 describes some of the characteristics of people who haven't been practicing authenticity, integrity, and creativity in their lives, and so they feel incomplete. How many of those words in the left-hand column described you when you first opened this book? Do they still fit? How many of the words in the right-hand column more aptly describe how you feel now? As you read this section, keep these questions in mind.

I don't mean to suggest that a fundamental transformation of your personality could have taken place, especially so quickly. But I do expect that you are starting to see yourself in a new light. Your sense of your potential as a leader changes as you learn more about yourself, about what you can do to get important things done, and about how to do so in a way that has the parts of your life in harmony. This, in turn, stimulates the desire to continue stretching, and having an impact beyond what you might have had in the past.

Now, as we finish up, to help you see what's changed in you as a result of your efforts, let's think further about what you wrote earlier in this chapter, and consider what it means for your authenticity, integrity and creativity. To help you do so, you'll read some of what participants have told me since they finished their initial experience with the Total Leadership course. When we're done, I'll ask you to look forward to what you'll do next and, finally, give you tips on how to tell the story of your achievement here in way that will help you grow while inspiring others.

### Authenticity—Feeling More Purposeful, Genuine, and Grounded

People change when they clarify what's important—they become more real. But authenticity is not just about you. Being a leader must involve others. As a leader, you drive performance in yourself and in the people you lead. You have to create commitment. You do that by demonstrating your own passion about a vision that is a compelling image of an achievable future.

It's your belief in what you're pursuing that binds people to your leadership vision and makes them want to go with you on the path you've identified, as André felt as he began moving toward his dream for black-owned enterprises. Since her last class session, Jenna had been concentrating on experiments that focus her attention and energy on her new priorities. As she explains it, she "consciously recognized as legitimate" her values, and now she acts accordingly. When she started my class, she felt unfocused. Now she feels more fully engaged, with herself and with her stakeholders. She has what she calls a greater "sense of purpose," and she tells me that by talking with others about what she's trying to accomplish, she feels "as if I'm being myself with them. And that feels good."

Ismail told me how he looks forward to the challenge of continually trying to find creative ways of doing what he loves. He has been tremendously successful in business and has made a lot of money, but he had never really felt *inspired* in his work or at home. Now, he inspires himself and others. Kerry changed jobs, from marketing executive to management consultant, and she told me that this had resulted in a tremendous improvement in all parts of her life. "My domains were almost stand-alone items prior to my Total Leadership experience, only slightly overlapped. I feel now that, with my job change, I have greater alignment with what I do in my work. And I spend more energy on myself and devote more attention to my friends."

*What would you say about your ability to act with authenticity now and about whether you're feeling more purposeful, genuine, and grounded than when you started this book?*

### Integrity—Feeling More Connected, Supported, and Resilient

The coherent sense of your life that comes from respecting the whole person can be transformational. The Total Leadership experience forces you to seek ways to bring the pieces together and help others achieve this, too. Part of doing so requires that you negotiate boundaries, limits that enable you to focus on results that matter, with all your key stakeholders. Both Roxanne and Ismail, for example, did this in experiments to bound and protect time with their children.

A primary goal of this book is to help you discover that you don't have to feel resentful of the push and pull of others, fragmented by the disparate nature of your life domains, and overwhelmed by what you have to navigate each day. Being whole is *not* about balancing by trading off one domain against another, as Victor told me recently.

> I've learned how limited you are when you try to achieve "work/life balance." That's an untenable approach. It's too simplistic. I'm now mindful that if I've got a choice of embarking on something new, no matter how small, it will always be of greater benefit if it's going to have a positive effect on more than one domain, rather than being just about work—which in the past was usually the case.

Thinking about how the different domains of your life are affecting each other—in other words, thinking about the integrity of your life—is one of the most important lessons you can draw from reading this book. You've been learning how to take a new perspective, one that encourages you to look for ways of integrating the different parts rather than trading one for another. Roxanne said:

> At the core of how I now think of myself as a leader is seeing how the activities most important to me don't have to compete with each other. Corporate work/life programs always focus on time, but it's a mistake to buy into this notion of time as the ultimate measure. Leadership is really about what you do with your time. It's powerful to find out that you don't have to trade things off, that you can get a lot of satisfaction out of seeing how what you

do here, in one part of your life, affects what happens over there, in that other part.

Very few of us can make it on our own, and for those of us who need to be reminded of this (especially men, it seems) and who then take action to build supportive connections, the results go well beyond just feeling better about ourselves. Our clients and coworkers see it and feel it, too. Lim told me that a big part of his new identity as a leader has to do with the "two-way" street of relationships.

With a large enough network of support that you build by being a good citizen in your various communities, you'll always have access to either someone who has encountered the very challenge you're facing or someone who knows someone who has. By tapping into that network, I've found amazing solutions to problems that seemed unsolvable.

Strengthening the feeling of closeness with people occurs when you reveal aspects of yourself through stories about what's happened in your life. It's not manipulation when you tell a story with the intent of increasing the sense of connection; it's leadership, because even though it's about you, it's really about the relationship, if you're doing it right. Total Leadership participants often describe to me how they come to realize that their lives essentially revolve around their key stakeholders. It becomes a clearer priority to build those connections.

Even in the most intimate relationships—perhaps especially in them— it's critical for you to keep channels of communication open to remain aware of expectations and how they change as life evolves. No matter how well you think you know a person, you never fully know about his or her expectations until you ask. Roxanne said that one of the most important aspects of her new way of thinking about leadership comes from getting feedback from stakeholders, what she called "hearing the voice of the customer," applying this marketing concept to how she needed to listen to all the important people around her. Many participants find that when they actually check to find out what people really expect of them, they discover that they have a lot more room to maneuver than they thought they had. They feel freer to choose a focus and so to take greater control of their lives. Such adjustment happens with stakeholders in all domains. The realizations allow you to refocus on critical people and projects. This is why participants are able to improve their ability to work smarter, and why they're producing stronger results for their customers, organizations, families, communities, and selves.

*What would you say about your ability to act with integrity now and about whether you're feeling more connected, supported, and resilient than when you started this book?*

### Creativity—Feeling More Curious, Engaged, and Optimistic

Victor recently told me about a new experiment he's got going at the bank where he's an IT director. He started it after he completed my Total Leadership course, but it builds on something he worked on in one of his original experiments. This new initiative shows how he has continued to experiment with how to get things done, how he's now more open to discovery and less stressed as a result.

When experiments evolve, as Victor's did, they demonstrate learning. They show a leader who is actively responsive to new opportunities and new needs that are discovered as he takes small steps toward creating something that hasn't existed before. Each step in a new direction puts you in a different position, one from which you see things with a fresh perspective, a new horizon. This process of initiating innovation, of experimenting, of being open to discovery, should never really end.

Roxanne described one of the ways in which she's working to build leadership capacity in herself and in others, simultaneously, by continuing to experiment.

> One experiment had to do with how I spend my lunchtime at work. I wanted to find a way to use that time to mentor and be mentored. Now, two years later, I'm in a new group that doesn't take regular breaks for lunch. But I do, and I also arrange lunches with people outside of my natural work team so I can learn something from them and they can hear something new from me.

Finding new ways to engage with others strengthens the bonds that make an organization's wheels go around. And by creating opportunities to reinforce ties beyond her normal work group, Roxanne's making her world a bit better connected.

Something Lim told me underscores the importance of overcoming the inhibitions that can slow you down, and Lim took important steps toward doing this in his life: "A key insight for me was that it's critical to have an attitude of openness to trying new things. It's like the Japanese word used in lean manufacturing: *kaizen*. Continuous improvement, I've come to realize, turns out to be fundamental to leadership, too." People who are learning are interested in the future.

André spoke of the optimism that flows from his new view of himself as a leader.

> I have learned the value of going from reflection to reprioritizing, planning, and acting—with creativity as a guiding principle. The process of routinely going through these steps allows me to maintain clarity of thought and direction. As long as I choose to do this, I'll keep myself on track, moving in the direction I truly want to go as a leader.

*What would you say about your ability to act with creativity now and about whether you're feeling more curious, engaged, and optimistic than when you started this book?*

## Next Steps in Your Development

Now that you've thought about what you've learned and how you've changed, it's useful to think more specifically about what you'll do to continue to grow as a leader. How will you keep the openness and inquiry of a student? Can you integrate lessons enough to teach or coach others?

---

### YOUR DEVELOPMENT AS STUDENT AND COACH

What are the two or three things you should keep in mind in the next year or so to continue your growth as a leader in all parts of your life?

What is the major obstacle you face in maintaining the momentum you've been able to build through your work in this book, and how do you intend to deal with it?

How would you coach someone about what you've learned here? What advice would you offer to people who might be thinking of embarking on their own Total Leadership learning journey?

Write notes on these questions, and talk them over with your coaches, friends, or other trusted advisers. Just as with your experiments, the more you let others know about your plans, the more likely they are to be realized because you'll feel more accountable and you'll get more support.

Leaders invent themselves by continually learning; it's an ongoing process. So it's useful to refresh your goals periodically, for they are likely to change over time. Here's what Lim thought about his learning agenda, the new goals that became his new baseline—the two or three key elements of his leadership development plan for the next few years: "First, keep striving to be the best father and husband I can be. Second, build on the lessons I've learned. Third, apply what I've learned in my new job." Simple to say, but it takes commitment to implement.

André, perhaps like you, realized that he was going to have to stay focused on learning as his educational needs changed over time:

> The major obstacle I'll face is the importance of recognizing there is no end, only a continual process of change and realignment. I can see down the road thinking to myself that I've "arrived," like the young kung fu student who was able to finally grab the pebble from the hand of the master. When that happens, I'm going to re-mind myself that it's time to reinvent, refocus, and realign.

He planned to keep sharp by teaching others some of the things he'd learned: "I'm going to share the experiments concept with others and be a role model through continuing to have honest dialogues with stake-holders, discussing goals and expectations." Having spent time reflecting on lessons learned and how to use them, Total Leadership participants are usually eager to offer words of wisdom about carrying forward the lessons they've learned in the form of teaching points to make with oth ers. Kerry advised "getting to the core. Don't take the easy way out, and do the first thing that comes to mind. Find those innovations that either truly represent an aligned scenario or get you down the path of ulti-mately aligning your domains. Try something new. Think through your leadership vision and have your experiments be the first step toward that vision."

Good advice. What would you say to your friends, work associates, or family?

Here's what Roxanne planned to say: "Focus too much on one domain, and you're probably not doing productive things. You might actually be doing destructive things. I used to marvel when reading about leaders, and wondering how they ever had time for all that they do. But it no longer seems unrealistic to me." And Victor's advice was this: "Go for the small wins. It's better not to go for the huge win and fail. Your successes will build upon each other." The important thing is to derive lessons that you want to transmit because, among other good reasons, in doing so you advance your own learning. Coaching others gives you new insight about your own unfolding development as a leader. And it can be inspiring to see what other people do to grow and create meaningful change in their lives.

## Tell Your Story

As we saw in chapter 2, effective leaders create emotional connections to the people around them by telling true stories that link their own personal experience to the needs and aspirations of others. If it's done well, a good leadership story will propel you forward in the direction you've chosen for the next steps of your leadership journey.

By telling the story of your experiments, and what you've learned from their design and implementation, you're in a better position to build ongoing support for change—for both existing experiments and future innovations—among the people in your networks, in your world. And it's a great way to teach what you know.

Keep telling your leadership stories to friends, family, and coworkers. Telling real stories about the events that have shaped your values—and about the kind of world you're trying to create—can strengthen

## TELL YOUR STORY

A good leadership story has the power to engage hearts and minds. It has these elements:

- Draws on your own past and lessons learned from it
- Engages the audience through emotional connection because of its relevance to them
- Inspires others because it's fueled by your passion
- Displays the struggle between your goal and obstacles you faced in achieving it
- Illustrates with vivid examples
- Teaches an important lesson

Sketch a story based on what you've been thinking and writing about here in the last part of this book, doing your best to bring each of the six elements above to life. Then find someone to whom you can relate your story. After you tell it, ask them what impact it had on them.

relationships with the people who matter most in your life. When I tell the story of my becoming a father and the impact this had on reshaping my career aspirations and leadership vision, it almost always brings me closer to the audience and helps them to see me as more accessible and credible. In part, that's because I'm describing a basic human experience to which the audience can relate. And I'm recounting a conscious choice I made to change my career, despite the resistance I then faced. But most of all, it's because the story is true and I'm passionate about it; it means a lot to me, and I believe that it has some value for others.

## Cultivate the Garden

As much as the world changes, we still face the twin challenges of finding the resources we must have to survive while trying to live in a way that has meaning. Through your work in this book, I hope you've gotten better at both these primary tasks.

Let me sum up by drawing a simple analogy, asking you to take a moment to imagine yourself as someone who, like most of the people who've come before us, works the land to live. As a leader, after all, you're a lot like a farmer. Your ideas for making things better in your world are the seeds of your crops. These seeds are within you, having grown ripe for planting during the course of your life. Through your intentional action, you bring them into the world.

You've got to till the soil to make it ready, just as you started this book by reflecting on where you are now and how you got here. You've then got to provide light, air, and water to help your seeds grow, just as you need to find support and nourishing resources to move your innovative ideas forward. Bringing your seeds of change into your key stakeholders' hearts and minds increases the chances that they will grow, that they will come true. And you've got to prune out the weeds, just as you need to give priority to the most important activities over others.

Your fields are sustainable to the extent that they don't require you to use more resources than you can afford. And they are sustaining if what they provide enriches you. Sustainable changes brought about by leaders are those that last because they aren't draining. Sustaining changes, however, like the most powerful Total Leadership experiments, are even better; they not only fit in without draining resources, they feed and enrich your world.

Of course it's hard to cultivate a field of crops or even a small garden. You have to really want to grow things to persist—in spite of all kinds of environmental threats, not to mention bad seeds—just as you've got to make a deliberate choice to lead, despite the risks, resistance, and unforeseeable obstacles. Most students of Total Leadership don't change their core values; but they do think and act differently—that is, with stronger conviction—about pursuing the things that matter most.

My purpose has been to help you increase your capacity to perform in ways that create value for all aspects of your life. If the ideas in this book are successfully cultivated, then everyone grows and everyone wins. If you take a whole-person view of leadership, in other words, you inevitably come to see that your actions as a leader can, indeed must, serve a larger purpose—a societal good—that moves us all forward. It's not hard to imagine, then, the purpose of leadership as getting ourselves back to the proverbial garden. I hope this book has in some way led to your feeling more a part of something that's bigger than your own life and that you have found greater meaning in what you do with your life as a result.

Among the things I most cherish about being a college professor are the rituals we have to mark cycles in the academic world, reflecting the seasonal rhythms of the natural world. Convocation starts it off—at which the novitiates are encouraged by smart old folks to engage themselves fully in discovery. Then, at the end, there's a ceremony to mark completion, paradoxically called "commencement." Just as James Joyce's great modern epic *Finnegans Wake* starts with the end of the last sentence, the end is the beginning of any important journey. Thank you for taking me along on this part of yours. Now, let's get started.

It's time to be a better leader, to have a richer life.

# Your Total Leadership
# Coaching Network

W HETHER YOU FORM ONE on your own or find one at
www.totalleadership.org, being in a coaching network
enhances the value of your Total Leadership experience. You can use
a coaching network to bring you the benefits of being both a coach and
a client (the term I prefer to describe the person receiving input from a
coach) in a learning community dedicated to producing four-way wins.

Coaching helps others improve performance now while developing
their capacity to perform well in the future. The specific benefits of being
a part of a community of coaches include:

- Support that enhances your confidence in trying new
  approaches

- Encouragement for intelligent risk taking in your experiments

- Specific suggestions for actions to achieve important results

- Increased accountability and, therefore, sustainability of changes you produce

- Improved ability to give and receive coaching support

- Camaraderie and a sense of belonging

Because the process of change is difficult and can provoke anxiety, people resist it. The forces of inertia can be strong, but good coaching helps overcome them. Perhaps most important of all, coaching feels good. Coaching is enjoyable because it's about learning. And it's even more fun and feels even better when you're on the giving end.

Before we go further, though, it's important to note that I'm not suggesting that you become a professional coach. What this appendix offers are tips and ideas to help you and your friends, colleagues, and family members use some basic coaching concepts and methods to enhance your experience of Total Leadership. But your Total Leadership coaching network is not a replacement for professional coaching or counseling support, which should be sought when problems in any aspect of your life reach the point where you are unable to deal effectively with them with your current resources.

## How Coaching Helps

Coaches provide support and accountability through both written and verbal input—questions, comments, and suggestions—about your work on the Total Leadership exercises. Throughout the process, they offer new insights, provide useful feedback, and encourage you to move toward your ideal. As a coach, you do the same for your clients.

We are often required to invest in helping others develop, offering constructive feedback, and inspiring others to experiment and take smart risks. When you coach someone, you get new ideas about your own leadership, in your work and in your life beyond work, while giving support to someone else. Total Leadership coaching offers a mutually beneficial experience for both coach and client for broadening skills.

Coaching can be either directive or nondirective. Directive coaching involves listening to your client and then offering advice from your own experiences or knowledge base. Nondirective coaching requires listening to your client's problems, but instead of then offering advice, asking questions that encourage your client to reach solutions independently. Asking good questions helps your client achieve greater self-understanding. Both forms of coaching can be effective; the preferred type depends on client needs. Participants who choose to make coaching a part of their Total Leadership experience can improve their capacity to give and receive all forms of support.

### Coaches Help You Be Real

Your coaches gain an understanding of where you're going, where you've been, and how things are now: your core values, experiences that have changed your life, whether your focus of time and attention fits with what's important to you, your leadership vision, and so on. They give you ideas to align your actions more closely with your leadership vision and your values, and challenge you to think creatively, question assumptions, and take intelligent risks. Coaches help you understand the choices you make that affect your work, home, community, and self. Coaching can have a powerful impact on how you think about what's important to you.

### Coaches Help You Be Whole

Coaches can help you understand the dynamics of your social world by asking questions and offering comments on your stakeholder analyses and on your preparation for and interpretation of your stakeholder dialogues. Coaching exchanges can play an important role in ensuring that you get the most value from these crucial conversations with the most important people in your life.

Coaches help you understand how you and your stakeholders fit in the complex web of your closest relationships. They help you better understand mutual expectations and shared interests, and they sense the potential for building stronger connections and improving performance by capitalizing on areas of common ground. Coaches push you to think through ideas for experiments gleaned from the information you take away from your stakeholder dialogues. They provide an objective—and usually refreshing—point of view to spur deeper exploration of how your key stakeholders affect your life and work.

### Coaches Help You Be Innovative

Coaches provide feedback about your experiments, from design through implementation and interpretation. They spur you to think seriously about new ways to approach work as an integral part of your life. Coaches can help design experiments that help you work smarter. They help you determine when to blend and when to bound domains. Coaches offer ideas on how to create metrics to measure both short- and long-term results. As commitment might falter when you meet resistance, coaches bolster you by problem solving with you and by urging you to carry through, to take steps in the direction in which you've chosen to grow.

## Create Your Coaching Network

To create your own coaching network, start by thinking about the people in your current personal and professional networks with whom you'd like to collaborate. They might be coworkers, friends, or members of your family—anyone who will go through the Total Leadership experience with you. The ideal size for a coaching team is three people.

On your coaching team you'll have a chance to be both coach and client, benefiting from both roles. The primary challenge for a client is to remain open and manage reactions to feedback. A coach's responsibility is to identify strengths and clarify areas for improvement that address the client's goals and help to reduce his or her defensiveness. Try to gain an understanding of your client's key relationships at work, at home, and in the community. At the same time, respect privacy and preferences for how much your client is willing to disclose.

It starts, then, with the three of you finding a time to talk about your goals. Expressing your goals increases the likelihood of obtaining them. The more open you are about your goals, the more likely they'll be realized, because your commitment will be higher. The chances of achieving goals increase when people provide mutual support. In this first conversation, you should also talk about your hopes and fears, and discuss what you wrote about your goals, in chapter 1.

This is also the time to discuss how the team will work together. You need to establish expectations, set up times to meet (via e-mail, phone, or face-to-face), and begin to learn about each other's working styles. The three of you would then each take the following steps:

1. Separately complete chapters 2 and 3 and distribute an electronic copy or just post it in a password-protected online group.

2. Read and comment on the other two members' work.

3. Read the comments written by the other two coaching team members.

4. Meet as a team, either in person or in real time by voice or video, to ask questions and discuss ideas, suggestions, and other reactions.

Repeat steps 1–4 for the second and third parts of the book.

## Effective Feedback

The essence of coaching is feedback. This is a gift, one that is best given straightforwardly and kindly. The quality and sensitivity of a coach's feedback can make a huge difference in your own growth. You produce value as a coach in helping your client to create meaningful change when you give feedback that:

- Addresses goals that are a real priority for the client

- Stretches your client to go as far as he or she can

- Asks questions that help clear up ambiguities

- Is balanced, not overly positive or negative

- Is communicated directly and specifically

- Offers constructive suggestions and ideas for improvements

- Is checked for clarity, to ensure that everyone understands what's being conveyed

- Offers follow-up assistance by leaving the door open for future coaching

## Helping Clients Meet the Challenges of Change

Many people fear change because it forces them into unknown territory, where things are unpredictable and unfamiliar. Total Leadership participants are challenged to innovate, to learn about themselves and others. The changes they undergo throughout the process can be uncomfortable. It's useful to know about the predictable stages people go through when they undertake intentional change. Below are these stages, as well as questions you can ask when your clients face the challenges of each particular stage.

### Awareness of the Need for Change

The first step is identifying the need for change. This can be difficult, as many of us ignore information that disconfirms our current perceptions or threatens the status quo. Total Leadership exercises are intended to increase self-awareness. Coaches can help identify blind spots—by encouraging self-reflection about things that aren't obvious to their clients. Key questions coaches should ask to increase awareness are:

- What's working and what isn't?

- How can you improve?

- What is the source of the need to change—is it in you or is it external?

### Sense of Urgency

Does it really matter whether the client changes? The next stage is about the belief that the need to change is urgent enough to take action. Because we tend toward inertia, if doing something new doesn't feel urgent, it's not likely to occur. Coaches can help by asking questions such as these:

- How important is your need to change?

- What will happen if you don't change?

- What will happen if you do change?

### Decision to Act

The decision to change is a crucial moment because it marks the point when your mind shifts and you begin to see a different future. It is also a fragile point in planned change processes. This point is fraught with temptations, diversions, and distractions. However, coaches can help participants reach this point by asking:

- What have you decided to do differently and why?

- What is the ideal outcome?

- What are your new goals?

## Problem Solving

What are the possible actions the client can take to make this decision something real in his or her work and in other parts of life? Coaches ask clients to think aloud about what to do differently, how to overcome obstacles, and what skills or sources of support are needed. In Total Leadership, coaches help design goals and metrics for experiments and talk through the nuts and bolts of producing small wins. Coaches can offer specific suggestions on how clients can better accomplish goals, asking:

- What exactly will you do, and when will you do it?

- How will you measure progress?

- What stands in the way?

- How will you overcome barriers or resistance?

- How will you generate needed support?

- How will you measure your success?

## Commitment

Generating sufficient commitment to follow through is one of the most challenging aspects of any change process. Because commitment wanes without a sense of urgency, coaches should continually test for this. Coaches can ask:

- Do you really have the will to go forward?

- What will happen to your commitment over time?

- What if this is harder than you think?

- What are the first steps—and the next steps—you will take?

- How will you sustain the will?

### Reinforcement

Even when a client has achieved all of the prior steps, it is crucial that he or she receive reinforcement for the positive outcomes gained. Encouraging every small step builds momentum, and coaches should repeatedly provide reinforcement and celebrate their clients' successes to bolster confidence and help clients avoid slippage. The key questions here are:

- What impact has your new behavior had on you and others?

- What accomplishments are you proud of achieving?

- Are you doing what you said you'd do?

- Is there a smarter step that might help you build momentum?

- How can I reinforce your commitment to action?

## Dos and Don'ts

Here are some tips on becoming an effective Total Leadership coach.

### Things to Do

- Show you care about helping your clients achieve their goals.

- Clarify coach and client roles through negotiation, and adjust expectations as needed.

- Share your own experiences only to help the client feel accepted, not to focus on you.

- Be as aware as possible of your own biases as a coach.

- Stay in touch with the reality your client is facing—listen well.

- Access your ignorance—ask questions, even ones you might think are dumb.

- Encourage your client to get help when needed, from all sources.

- If you cannot provide feedback at the time your client is expecting it, immediately communicate this to your client to explain the delay. This builds trust.

### *Things to Avoid Doing*

- Avoid inactivity, or not working at being a coach. Like any good relationship, coaching requires time, energy, and thoughtfulness by both participants.

- Don't criticize your client's ideas. Listen and offer alternatives.

- Don't promise more than you can deliver; this will decrease your credibility.

Virtually all Total Leadership program participants have found coaching to be beneficial and enjoyable. Many people still keep in touch with their coaches and stay updated on new developments in their work and personal lives. I hope you decide to create your own coaching network. As you continue to explore coaching in your own Total Leadership experience and beyond, I trust you'll find just how rewarding it can be.

Visit www.totalleadership.org for more information on Total Leadership coaching.

# Scoring Four-Way Wins with Total Leadership in Your Organization

T HIS BOOK is about how the Total Leadership program can benefit individuals. Similarly, in your organization, a Total Leadership program can improve performance, satisfaction, and alignment in employees' four life domains. As a result, your organization will increase its ability to innovative and to compete, while also improving talent retention and reducing health-care costs.

Your organization *is* your employees. The Total Leadership program provides a framework, a language, and a motivation for making positive change on every organizational level. It can result in people focusing more of their energy on the pursuit of business goals, thereby improving

morale, boosting efficiency, increasing resilience, fostering collaboration, and making work more engaging.

It's possible to achieve these aims in any kind of organization, of any
size and in any setting. However, the means for doing so depend on how
deeply felt the need for change is and how ready key decision makers
are to cultivate grassroots experimentation.

Just as no two participants take the same course through Total
Leadership, no two organizations do either. In every Total Leadership
program, the outcomes differ because the raw material—you, your
organization—is never the same. The key to achieving four-way wins
systemwide is to apply the same basic principles described in this book
to your entire organization.

## Be Real

The process starts with knowing what's important, being real about
your organization's aspirations. Whether the idea is introduced by a
frontline employee who's read this book or a CEO who heard about it
from a friend at a cocktail party, at some point—sooner is better than
later—top management must have an honest dialogue about what it
takes to experiment with four-way wins.

Just as individuals embarking on a Total Leadership journey
naturally feel some ambivalence, there will be resistance in your organization. But the business case isn't hard to make, because the main
purpose is mutual gain for all stakeholders. First and foremost in the
conversation, then, must be the understanding that the Total Leadership method is not about trading business success for satisfaction in
one's life outside of work but about experimenting with ways of demonstrably improving business results while at the same time improving
quality of life in the other three domains: home, community, and self. It
does not involve radical and wholesale programmatic shifts in HR policy

but, rather, incremental, data-driven learning, which is less threatening and much easier to manage.

## Be Whole

Achieving four-way wins is a sustainable and sustaining goal because it directly addresses the need for integrity, or wholeness, in a person's life. The practice of the Total Leadership method is a creative search for ways to meet the expectations of all key stakeholders, in all domains. It's the same for organizations. A successful Total Leadership program explicitly respects the interests of various constituencies: employees and their families, owners, managers, customers, clients, suppliers, local communities, and society.

Because the experiments conducted by organization members—following a serious consideration of stakeholder expectations—must address their four domains, the impact of these experiments accumulates. In a variety of ways throughout the organization, people design and implement experiments to make things better for all the organization's stakeholders. When disseminated throughout an organization, therefore, a Total Leadership program is not only a means for performance improvement and skill building, it is an opportunity to demonstrate corporate social responsibility in a way that is meaningful for each organization member.

## Be Innovative

Intelligent, low-risk experiments are the central activity of the Total Leadership process. The long-lasting takeaway from the process, after all, is that participants become better at creating and implementing productive change. When you have many people undertaking this effort in your organization, you produce a cultural context that sends a message of support for continual innovation, as long as you keep in mind that what might seem new and challenging to one group might seem conventional and simple to another. Indeed, this is a critical success factor: don't judge too harshly whether another's experiment is worthwhile.

The hardest part is just getting started. That's why the best approach is to run a pilot program and surround it with data about what's working and what must be adjusted to make the process work better. A pilot is low-cost and low-risk—a small-wins approach to large-scale change. Once you've got a group of employees who've done their own experiments, you're on your way to spreading knowledge and introducing a new way of thinking about leadership development and work/life integration, because now you've got people in your organization who can tell credible stories about real and positive change.

One example of Total Leadership in action comes from a global investment bank, which launched a pilot program—they called it "Four-Way Wins"—with a group of midlevel managers in its New York headquarters. The impetus behind the program came from the bank's commitment to evolving the culture to promote sustainable high performance and resilience. This commitment was reinforced by the bank's president and COO, who, driven by his own awareness and urgency to create a new leadership mind-set, joined the participants' debrief of the pilot program to explore the Four-Way Wins model.

The participants' managers attended the session to discuss the results of the initial experiments and lessons learned from them. Though some participants were unable to complete successful experiments, a significant number of them had, producing demonstrable gains. The participants and their managers talked about dealing with obstacles to change, defined conditions for success, and brainstormed ideas for providing further support for the next wave of participants.

Most importantly, the successful experiments built credibility and momentum for ongoing dialogue and forward movement, proving that four-way wins are possible even in a very intense work environment. Recognizing that practical adjustments in work methods can yield better results for the individual *and* for the business, the co-chief administrative officer and the global head of the bank's Investment Banking division continued to drive progress forward.

The overriding message from the top was this: We expect you to try new ways of getting things done and we will actively support your initiatives to do so. The pilot program, itself a smart experiment, paved the way for increased focus on the importance and feasibility of improving the quality of employees' lives outside of work while improving their performance at work, even for those who held extremely demanding jobs.

# Further Reading

THIS APPENDIX provides references for essential articles and books on topics covered in this book. They are organized according to six general categories.

## Leadership

Badaracco, J. L. *Defining Moments: When Managers Must Choose Between Right and Right*. Boston: Harvard Business School Press, 1997.

Bennis, W. G., and R. J. Thomas. *Geeks and Geezers: How Era, Values, and Defining Moments Shape Leaders*. Boston: Harvard Business School Press, 2002.

Boyatzis, R., and A. McKee. *Resonant Leadership: Renewing Yourself and Connecting with Others Through Mindfulness, Hope, and Compassion*. Boston: Harvard Business School Press, 2005.

Burns, J. M. *Transforming Leadership: The Pursuit of Happiness*. New York: Atlantic Monthly Press, 2003.

Collins, J. *Good to Great*. New York: HarperBusiness, 2001.

Drucker, P. F. "Managing Oneself." *Harvard Business Review*, January 2005, 1–10.

Finkelstein, S. *Why Smart Executives Fail*. New York: Penguin, 2003.

Friedman, S. D., and S. Lobel. "The Happy Workaholic: A Role Model for Employees." *Academy of Management Executive* 17, no. 3 (2003): 87.

Gardner, H. *Leading Minds*. New York: Basic Books, 1995.

Gardner, J. W. *On Leadership*. New York: Free Press, 1990.

Hoppe, M. H., and G. Houston. "A Question of Leadership: How Much of Themselves Should Leaders Bring to Their Work?" *Leadership in Action* 24, no. 3 (2004): 13.

Kotter, J. P. *Leading Change*. Boston: Harvard Business School Press, 1996.

Kouzes, J. M., and B. Z. Posner. *The Leadership Challenge: How to Keep Getting Extraordinary Things Done in Organizations*. San Francisco: Jossey-Bass, 1996.

Lorsch, J. W., and T. J. Tierney. *Aligning the Stars: How to Succeed When Professionals Drive Results*. Boston: Harvard Business School Press, 2002.

Raelin, J. A. *Creating Leaderful Organizations: How to Bring Out Leadership in Everyone*. San Francisco: Berrett-Koehler, 2003.

Ruderman, M. N., and P. J. Ohlott. *Standing at the Crossroads: Next Steps for High-Achieving Women*. San Francisco: Jossey-Bass, 2002.

Seligman, M. E. P. *Authentic Happiness: Using the New Positive Psychology to Realize Your Potential for Lasting Fulfillment*. New York: Free Press, 2002.

Thomas, D. A., and J. J. Gabarro. *Breaking Through: The Making of Minority Executives in Corporate America*. Boston: Harvard Business School Press, 1999.

Tichy, N. *The Leadership Engine*. New York: HarperBusiness, 2002.

Tzu, S. *The Art of War*. Edited and with Foreword by J. Clavell. New York: Dell, 1983.

Useem, M. *The Leadership Moment*. New York: Times Business, 1998.

## How Domains of Life Affect Each Other

Ashforth, B. E., G. E. Kreiner, and M. Fugate. "All in a Day's Work: Boundaries and Micro Role Transitions." *Academy of Management Review*, 25, no. 3 (2000): 472.

Drago, R. W. *Striking a Balance: Work, Family, Life*. Boston: Dollars & Sense, 2007.

Edwards, J. R., and N. P. Rothbard. "Mechanisms Linking Work and Family: Clarifying the Relationship Between Work and Family Constructs." *Academy of Management Review*, 25, no. 1 (2000): 178.

Friedman, S. D., and J. H. Greenhaus. *Work and Family—Allies or Enemies? What Happens When Business Professionals Confront Life Choices*. New York: Oxford University Press, 2000.

Frone, M. R., R. M. Marcia, and L. Cooper. "Prevalence of Work-Family Conflict: Are Work and Family Boundaries Asymmetrically Permeable?" *Journal of Organizational Behavior* 13, no. 7 (1992): 723.

Greenhaus, J. H., and G. Powell. "When Work and Family Are Allies: A Theory of Work-Family Enrichment." *Academy of Management Review* 31 (2006): 72–92.

Hall, D. T., and V. A. Parker. "The Role of Workplace Flexibility in Managing Diversity." *Organizational Dynamics* 22, no. 1 (1993): 4.

Hammonds, K. "Balance Is Bunk!" *Fast Company*, October 2004, 68–76.

Katz, D., and R. L. Kahn. *The Social Psychology of Organizations.* 2nd ed. New York: John Wiley & Sons, 1978.

Kossek, E. E., R. A. Noe, and B. J. DeMarr. "Work-Family Role Synthesis: Individual and Organizational Determinants." *International Journal of Conflict Management* 10, no. 2 (1999): 102.

Nippert-Eng, C. E. *Home and Work: Negotiating Boundaries Through Everyday Life.* Chicago: University of Chicago Press, 1996.

Perlow, L. A. "Boundary Control: The Social Ordering of Work and Family Time in a High-Tech Corporation." *Administrative Science Quarterly* 43, no. 2 (1998): 328.

Rothbard, N. P. "Enriching or Depleting? The Dynamics of Engagement in Work and Family Roles." *Administrative Science Quarterly* 46, no. 4 (2002): 655.

Shellenbarger, S. *Work and Family: Essays from the "Work and Family" Column of the Wall Street Journal.* New York: Ballantine Books, 1999

Siegel, P. A., C. Post, J. Brockner, A. Y. Fishman, and C. Garden. "The Moderating Influence of Procedural Fairness on the Relationship Between Work-Life Conflict and Organizational Commitment." *Journal of Applied Psychology* 90, no. 1 (2005): 13.

## Connecting with Stakeholders: Communication, Networks, and Politics

Baker, W. *Achieving Success Through Social Capital.* San Francisco: Jossey-Bass, 2000.

Christensen, P. M., and B. L. Porter. *Family 360: A Proven Approach to Getting Your Family to Talk, Solve Problems, and Improve Relationships.* New York: McGraw-Hill, 2004.

Cialdini, R. B. *Influence: The Psychology of Persuasion*. New York: William Morrow, 1993.

Cohen, D., and L. Prusak. *In Good Company: How Social Capital Makes Organizations Work*. Boston: Harvard Business School Press, 2001.

DeLuca, J. *Political Savvy: Systematic Approaches to Leadership Behind-the-Scenes*. Berwyn, PA: EBG Publications, 1999.

Ferrazzi, K. *Never Eat Alone*. New York: Currency/Doubleday, 2005.

Fisher, R., W. Ury, and P. Patton. *Getting to Yes: Negotiating Agreement Without Giving In*. New York: Penguin Books, 1991.

Gabarro, J. J., and J. P. Kotter. "Managing Your Boss." *Harvard Business Review*, May 1993, 150–157.

Hallowell, E. M. *Connect: 12 Vital Ties That Open Your Heart, Lengthen Your Life, and Deepen Your Soul*. New York: Pocket Books, 1999.

Hanson, J. *More Than 85 Broads*. New York: McGraw-Hill, 2006.

Pfeffer, J. *Managing with Power: Politics and Influence in Organizations*. Boston: Harvard Business School Press, 1992.

Scott, S. *Fierce Conversations: Achieving Success at Work and in Life, One Conversation at a Time*. New York: Viking, 2002.

Shell, G. R. *Bargaining for Advantage*. New York: Penguin, 1999.

Shell, G. R., and M. Moussa. *The Art of Woo*. New York: Penguin, 2007.

Useem, M. *Leading Up: How to Lead Your Boss So You Both Win*. New York: Crown Business/Random House, 2001.

Watts, D. J. *Six Degrees: The Science of a Connected Age*. New York: W. W. Norton & Company, 2003.

## Coaching and Leadership Education

Boyatzis, R. E., S. S. Cowen, and D. A. Kolb. *Innovation in Professional Education: Steps on a Journey from Teaching to Learning: The Story of Change and Invention at the Weatherhead School of Management*. San Francisco: Jossey-Bass, 1994.

Caproni, P. J. *The Practical Coach: Management Skills for Everyday Life*. Upper Saddle River, NJ: Prentice Hall, 2001.

Conger, J. A., and B. Benjamin. *Building Leaders: How Successful Companies Develop the Next Generation*. San Francisco: Jossey-Bass, 1999.

Fryer, B. "Storytelling That Moves People: A Conversation with Screenwriting Coach Robert McKee." *Harvard Business Review*, June 2003, 5–8.

Ghoshal, S. "Bad Management Theories Are Destroying Good Management Practices." *Academy of Management Learning and Education*, 4, no. 1 (2005): 75.

Ibarra, H. *Working Identity: Unconventional Strategies for Reinventing Your Career*. Boston: Harvard Business School Press, 2003.

McCall, M. W., M. M. Lombardo, and A. M. Morrison. *The Lessons of Experience: How Successful Executives Develop on the Job*. Lexington, MA: Lexington Books, 1988.

McCauley, C. D., R. S. Moxley, and E. Van Velsor, eds. *The Center for Creative Leadership Handbook of Leadership Development*. San Francisco: Jossey-Bass, 1998.

Mintzberg, H. *Managers, Not MBAs: A Hard Look at the Soft Practice of Managing and Management Development*. San Francisco: Berrett-Koehler, 2004.

Mirvis, P., and L. Gunning. "Creating a Community of Leaders." *Organizational Dynamics* 35, no. 1 (2006): 69.

Pfeffer, J., and R. I. Sutton. "Evidence-Based Management." *Harvard Business Review*, January 2006, 62.

Ragins, B. R., and K. E. Kram (eds.). *The Handbook of Mentoring at Work: Theory, Research, and Practice*. Thousand Oaks, CA: Sage Publications, 2007

Rousseau, D. M. "Is There Such a Thing as 'Evidence-Based' Management?" *Academy of Management Review*, 31:2, April 2006, pp. 256–269

Schein, E. H. *Process Consultation Revisited. Building the Helping Relationship*. Reading, MA: Addison-Wesley, 1999.

Tichy, N. M. *The Cycle of Leadership: How Great Leaders Teach Their Companies to Win*. New York: HarperBusiness, 2002.

## Leading Change to Integrate Work and Other Domains of Life

Bailyn, L. *Breaking the Mold: Redesigning Work for Productive and Satisfying Lives*. 2nd ed. Ithaca, NY: ILR Press, 2006.

Barnett, R. C., and C. Rivers. *She Works/He Works: How Two-Income Families Are Happier, Healthier, and Better Off*. San Francisco: HarperSanFrancisco, 1996.

Burud, S. L., and M. Tumolo. *Leveraging the New Human Capital: Adaptive Strategies, Results Achieved, and Stories of Transformation*. Palo Alto, CA: Davies-Black Publishing, 2004.

Cappelli, P. *The New Deal at Work: Managing the Market-Driven Workforce*. Boston: Harvard Business School Press, 1999.

Dutton, J. E. *Energize Your Workplace: How to Create and Sustain High-Quality Connections at Work*. New York: John Wiley & Sons, 2003.

Friedman, S. D. "Leadership DNA: The Ford Motor Story." *Training and Development* 55, no. 3 (2001): 22.

Friedman, S. D., P. Christensen, and J. DeGroot. "Work and Life:

The End of the Zero-Sum Game." *Harvard Business Review*, November 1998, 119.

Galinsky, E. *Ask the Children: What America's Children Really Think About Working Parents*. New York: William Morrow, 1999.

Googins, B. K. "Work, Families, and Organizations." *Industrial and Labor Relations Review* 47, no. 2 (1994): 345.

Hall, D. T., and B. Harrington. *Career Management & Work/Life Integration: Using Self-Assessment to Navigate Contemporary Careers*. Thousand Oaks, CA: Sage Publications, 2007.

Hewlett, S. A., and C. West. *The War Against Parents: What We Can Do for America's Beleaguered Moms and Dads*. Boston: Houghton Mifflin, 1998.

Huston, P. *Families As We Are: Conversations from Around the World*. New York: Feminist Press of the City University of New York, 2001.

Jacobs, J. A., and K. Gerson. *The Time Divide: Work, Family, and Gender Inequality*. Cambridge, MA: Harvard University Press, 2004.

Kanter, R. M. *Work and Family in the United States: A Critical Review and Agenda for Research and Policy*. New York: Russell Sage Foundation, 1977.

Loehr, J., and T. Schwartz. *The Power of Full Engagement*. New York: Free Press, 2003.

Mainiero, L. A., and S. E. Sullivan. *The Opt-Out Revolt: Why People Are Leaving Companies to Create Kaleidoscope Careers*. Mountain View, CA: Davies-Black Publishing, 2006.

Pitt-Catsouphes, M., E. E. Kossek, and S. Sweet, S., eds. *The Work and Family Handbook: Multi-Disciplinary Perspectives and Approaches*. Mahwah, NJ: Lawrence Erlbaum, 2006.

Presser, H. B. *Working in a 24/7 Economy: Challenges for American Families*. New York: Russell Sage Foundation, 2003.

Rothbard, N. P., K. W. Phillips, and T. L. Dumas. "Managing Multiple Roles: Work-Family Policies and Individuals' Desires for Segmentation." *Organization Science* 16, no. 3 (2005): 243.

Rousseau, D. M. *I-deals: Idiosyncratic Deals Employees Bargain for Themselves.* Armonk, NY: M. E. Sharpe, 2005.

Stone, P. *Opting Out? Why Women Really Quit Careers and Head Home.* Berkeley, CA: University of California Press, 2007.

Ulrich, D., and N. Smallwood. *Why the Bottom Line ISN'T! How to Build Value Through People and Organization.* New York: John Wiley & Sons, 2003.

Weick, K. E. "Small Wins: Redefining the Scale of Social Problems." *American Psychologist* 39, no. 1 (1984): 40–49.

## Social Impact and Spiritual Growth Through Leadership

Bolman, L. G., and T. E. Deal. *Leading with Soul: An Uncommon Journey of Spirit.* San Francisco: Jossey-Bass, 2001.

Bornstein, D. *How to Change the World. Social Entrepreneurs and the Power of New Ideas.* Oxford: Oxford University Press, 2004.

Conger, J. A. and Associates. *Spirit at Work: Discovering the Spirituality in Leadership.* San Francisco: Jossey-Bass, 1994.

Csikszentmihalyi, M. *Good Business: Leadership, Flow, and the Making of Meaning.* New York: Viking, 2003.

Gardner, H., M. Csikszentmihalyi, and W. Damon. *Good Work: When Excellence and Ethics Meet.* New York: Basic Books, 2001.

Greenleaf, R. K. *Servant Leadership: A Journey into the Nature of Legitimate Power & Greatness.* Mahwah, NJ: Paulist Press, 1977.

Heschel, A. J. *The Sabbath: It's Meaning for Modern Man.* New York: Farrar, Straus and Giroux, 1951.

Hollender, J., and S. Fenichell. *What Matters Most: How a Small Group of Pioneers Is Teaching Social Responsibility to Big Business, and Why Big Business Is Listening.* New York: Basic Books, 2004.

Mitroff, I. I., and E. A. Denton. *A Spiritual Audit of Corporate America: A Hard Look at Spirituality, Religion, and Values in the Workplace.* San Francisco: Jossey-Bass, 1999.

Pava, M. L. *Leading with Meaning: Using Covenantal Leadership to Build a Better Organization.* New York: Palgrave Macmillan, 2003.

Shellenbarger, S. "Drafted Volunteers: Employees Face Pressure to Work on Company Charities." *The Wall Street Journal*, November 20, 2003.

## Chapter 1

1. The finance department managers in their respective business units verified these numbers.

2. This was the main argument Sharon Lobel and I made in our 2003 article, "The Happy Workaholic: A Role Model for Employees," published in the *Academy of Management Executive* 17, no. 3 (2003): 87–98.

3. Some of these are described in a book I wrote with Jeff Greenhaus, *Work and Family—Allies or Enemies? What Happens When Business Professionals Confront Life Choices* (New York: Oxford University Press, 2000).

4. See appendix C, Further Reading, and visit www.totalleadership.org for more of the research underpinnings of the Total Leadership program.

5. Most influential were Daniel Katz and Robert Kahn, who wrote the field-defining *The Social Psychology of Organizations* (second edition). (New York: John Wiley & Sons, 1976).

6. The prime movers were Rosabeth Moss Kanter and Lotte Bailyn.

7. Friedman and Greenhaus, *Work and Family—Allies or Enemies?*

8. See, as examples, Noel M. Tichy's series of works on leadership development, for instance, *The Leadership Engine: How Winning Companies Build Leaders at Every Level* (New York: HarperCollins, 2002).

9. Led by Karl Weick.

10. Peter F. Drucker, "Managing Oneself," *Harvard Business Review*, January 2005, 1–10.

11. For example, by such scholars as Jeffrey Pfeffer, Denise Rousseau, and Robert Sutton, who appeal for evidence-based management.

## Chapter 2

1. Howard Gardner, *Leading Minds: An Anatomy of Leadership* (New York: Basic Books, 1995).

2. Steve Jobs, commencement address delivered at Stanford University, June 12, 2005.

3. Noel M. Tichy, *The Leadership Engine: How Winning Companies Build Leaders at Every Level* (New York: HarperCollins, 2002).

## Chapter 3

1. Stewart D. Friedman and Jeffrey H. Greenhaus, *Work and Family—Allies or Enemies? What Happens When Business Professionals Confront Life Choices* (New York: Oxford University Press, 2000).

## Chapter 5

1. G. Richard Shell, *Bargaining for Advantage: Negotiation Strategies for Reasonable People* (New York: Penguin, 1999).

## Chapter 6

1. Abraham Joshua Heschel, *The Sabbath: Its Meaning for Modern Man* (New York: Farrar, Straus and Giroux, 1951).

## Chapter 7

1. "Indra Nooyi: Keeping Cool in Hot Water," *BusinessWeek*, June 11, 2007.

2. Stewart D. Friedman and Jeffrey H. Greenhaus, *Work and Family—Allies or Enemies? What Happens When Business Professionals Confront Life Choices* (New York: Oxford University Press, 2000).

3. Joel R. DeLuca, *Political Savvy: Systematic Approaches to Leadership Behind the Scenes* (Berwyn, PA: EBG Publications, 1999).

4. Wayne E. Baker, *Achieving Success Through Social Capital* (San Francisco: Jossey-Bass, 2000).

5. Adapted from an exercise first developed by Wayne E. Baker; see humaxnetworks .com.

## ACKNOWLEDGMENTS

**M**ANY PEOPLE from different parts of my life have helped bring this book to life. To fully acknowledge all those who've contributed to it would be to write a detailed autobiography! But let me instead take a moment to thank those who've mattered most.

A thunderbolt hit me when I first laid eyes on Hallie Friedman (neé Boorstyn). Thankfully, I had the good sense to follow my heart to be with her at the University of Michigan and the good luck to succeed in persuading her to marry me. In every part of my life, including the creation of this book, she has been my inspiration, my guiding light, and the very source of my best.

At the University of Michigan I was truly blessed to have Bob Kahn and Noel Tichy as the cochairs of my dissertation research. Each of them showed me how to be a practical scholar, that it was a noble ideal to try to make the world a little better as an organizational psychologist. Bob's groundbreaking work on role theory inspired me, like many of his students, to seek useful knowledge about how work and the rest of life might be mutually enriching. Noel's wise counsel, his generous sponsorship, and his uncanny gift for leading change that serves organizations and society have continued to guide my development. If not for his intense, productive coaching and constant support for my efforts at Ford, the Total Leadership program would not be.

Other colleagues at Michigan, both students and faculty, taught me with their contagious passion that organizations could be made more fruitful as instruments for achieving richer lives; they include a diverse array of remarkably creative people who constituted my wonderfully supportive intellectual family of origin, especially Doug Cowherd, Dan Denison, J. Richard Hackman, Denise Rousseau, Marian Ruderman, Roger Schwarz, Stan Seashore, Bob Sutton, and Joe Veroff.

The Wharton School has been my professional home for over two decades, and it's here that I found my voice, with the encouragement of my colleagues and mentors. From the start of his tenure as dean, Tom Gerrity has been a generous supporter of my initiatives in both the work/life and leadership fields, providing the vision and resources needed to get both the Work/Life Integration Project and the Graduate and Undergraduate Leadership Programs off the ground. I am deeply appreciative for the faith that Tom and Janice Bellace—first as vice dean for our Undergraduate Division and then as Wharton's deputy dean—had in me. I'm grateful to Howie Kaufold, who gave me the chance to offer Total Leadership to the world-class students in our Executive MBA program. Many in the Management Department, and colleagues in other parts of Penn, have given invaluable support, most notably Sigal Barsade, Peter Cappelli, Doug Frenkel, Dwight Jaggard, John Kimberly, Katherine Klein, Marilyn Kraut, Dan Levinthal, Hans Pennings, Greg Shea, Harbir Singh, Jitendra Singh, Mike Useem, and Ross Webber.

I've had the great fortune of working with the best students one could possibly hope to have. I teach to learn, and they have been the greatest teachers. I'm indebted to them all, and particularly Amanda Abrams, Mia Adelberg, Kristine Martin Anderson, John Ballard, Po Chen, Amy Dahm, Jessica DeGroot, Ellen Hoch, Brett Hurt, Meredith Myers, Joe Piernock, Denise Shumway, Phyllis Siegel, Stu Silberman, Susan Sotiropoulos, Lucy Stribley, Harry Weiner, Jonathan Wells, Evan Wittenberg, and to every one of the students who worked through the rigors of the Total Leadership class, especially those who are the basis for the characters in this book and the source of its illustrative material.

I've been fortunate to have had many Wharton students serving on my research team who have contributed their immense energy and remarkable intelligence, especially Alex Chernyak, Sandip Garg, Phaedon Gourtsoyannis, Beeneet Kothari, Marina Pristupova, Tom Radford, Katie Semida, and Nana Xu. And I'm grateful to the members of my team from outside of Wharton for their help in building the Total Leadership program, especially Debbie Hufnagel, Erin Owen, and Stacey Radin.

I am extremely thankful for the opportunity I had to serve at the Ford Motor Company. Nothing in my experience has produced so many long-lasting lessons about life in organizations. It was because of the visionary leadership supplied by CEO Jacques Nasser and human resources chief David Murphy that I had the chance to experiment with new models of leadership education. It was an honor to work side by side with the inspiring members of this iconic company, and I continue to feel great pride in what our team at the Leadership Development Center accomplished. For their invaluable contributions to the development of Total Leadership I'm especially grateful to Nancy Atwood, Tom Grant, and Nerissa Morris.

But the mentor who did the most to coax the Total Leadership program out of me was Joel DeLuca, whom I first met when we worked together in the early days of Wharton's Graduate Leadership Program and who then consulted with our group at Ford. I am awed by his brilliance as an architect of social change and leadership development, and am very fortunate to have benefited from his true friendship and intellectual guidance.

The ideas in this book were shaped by my reading and talking with many scholars and practitioners in the fields of work/life and leadership. With some I have had the special privilege of serving as coauthor: Michelle Carpenter, Perry Christensen, Jessica DeGroot, Ellen Galinsky, Alyssa Friede, Hallie Friedman, Jeff Greenhaus, Sharon Lobel, Dennis Marcel, Paul Olk, Saroj Parasuraman, Kathleen Saul, Harbir Singh, Cynthia Thompson, Noel Tichy, and Dave Ulrich.

Ellen Galinsky and Dana Friedman, cofounders of the Families and Work Institute, have been beacons for me and powerful voices for progressive change in organizations and society. My work has benefited from Kathleen Christensen's leadership of the Alfred P. Sloan Foundation's Workplace, Work Force and Working Families program. And I've learned important lessons from many other work/life pacesetters, including Sandy Burud, Bob Carr, Roger Brown, Ted Childs, Brad Googins, Tim Hall, Deborah Holmes, Arlene Johnson, Donna Klein, Joan Kofodimos, Ellen Kossek, Kathie Lingle, Shelly MacDermid, Linda Mason, Denise Montana, Karol Rose, and Faith Wohl.

There are so many teachers and practitioners of the art of leadership to whom I owe much. These include Wayne Baker, Schon Beechler, Paula Caproni, Ken Eisold, Tom Gilmore, Al Gore, Janet Hanson, Jeff Hanson, Joe Harder, Herminia Ibarra, Larry Kessner, Phil Laskaway, Dave Lissy, Marc Margolius, Phil Mirvis, Simon Mordant, Moses Pava, Len Schlesinger, Stan Silverman, Sim Sitkin, Jeff Sonnenfeld, Andy Stefanovich, Anne Stevens, David Thomas, Tom Tierney, Jack Welch, Suzy Welch, Gary Weinstein, and Mitch Wienick.

I have had the privilege of applying this book's principles in some of the finest organizations in the world and have gained great insight from collaborations with many creative agents of change working inside them, including Shlomo Ben-Hur, Joy Bunson, Leora Cohen, Anne Erni, Sharon Gargano, Hildur Jónsdóttir, Sandra Lapp, Ken Lichtenstein, Laura Mendelow, Judith Maurer, Matt McElrath, Nancy Mellos, Rob Meyer, Vernita Parker-Wilkins, Farrell Redwine, Gwen Rosser, Nona Saling, Deborah Sheppe, and Jamie Turner.

I was lucky, in the 1980s, to seize on an issue about which many people were beginning to seek useful knowledge, and doubly so to be a man when most of the others generating such knowledge were women. Being different helped me to gain some visibility, but this would not have happened without pioneering journalists to tell the story. I would like to thank especially Keith Hammonds, Barbara Presley Noble, and Sue Shellenbarger for their courageous reportage.

I am very grateful to the amazing Melinda Merino, executive editor at the Harvard Business Press, for her patient support and brilliant editorial insight as she guided me through the long process of digging this book out from under a mountain of material. Jim Levine, my literary agent, has been a constant guide throughout the entire process of constructing this book. And were it not for the editorial support and penetrating wisdom graciously offered by both Scott Cooper and Connie Hale, I would have never have completed this journey.

In my community domain I have been blessed by the warm embrace of many friends who have enriched my life, supported me during difficult times, and informed my ideas for this book. I am deeply indebted to them all.

I want to thank my original family for their endless love: my parents, Leah and Victor Friedman, who have never stopped believing in me; my brother, Paul Ben-Victor, who has always shown me another side of myself; and my sister, Susan Schrott, who in looking up to me has inspired me. I am forever indebted to my father-in-law, Neil Doorstyn, one of the great legal minds, who has worked tirelessly to help me navigate many professional relationships

Gabriel, Harry, and Lody—my most precious stakeholders, for they *are* my future—hold the key to my heart and so make my life whole. To my great good fortune, I have the task of helping them to grow. They gave me the will to persist in finishing this book, which I hope in some small way will lead to their world being a little better, their lives a little richer.

# CHARACTER INDEX

*Note:* all names are disguised.

"Chang, Lim," 187
dialogue with "dreaded stakeholder,"
53–55
early efforts, 53–55
experimentation, 153–156
four circles review, 183–184
leadership lessons, 186
learning agenda, 195
overcoming inhibitions, 193
reflection on experiments, 172
relationship changes, 191

"Cohen, Mike," 125–126

"Garcia, Sally," 176

"Gardner, Victor," 187, 190
analysis of stakeholder expectations,
89–90
boundaries between domains, 85
core values, 49
experimentation, 153, 160, 192
four-way attention chart, 58–60,
63–64, 64 (*fig.*), 182, 183 (*fig.*)
identification of key stakeholders,
73–74, 77
leadership vision, 42–45

overcoming inhibitions, 89–90, 158
small wins, 196
stakeholder dialogues, 97–98
what he expects of key stakeholders,
83–84

"Hashemi, Ismail," 187, 189, 190
clarification of issues, 121–122
cultivating trust, 167
design of experiments, 122–123, 198
review of experiments, 173–175

"Miller, Mike," 110–111

"Pappas-Grant, Roxanne," 187
clarification of issues, 34–37
experimentation, 132–133, 136, 153,
193
four-way attention chart, 65–67, 66
(*fig.*)
integrating various domains, 190–191
leadership lessons, 185, 191–192, 196
reflection on experiments, 175–176
stakeholder dialogues, 113–114
stakeholder expectations review,
178–179
values and vision review, 181

"Porter, Jenna," 187, 189
  cultivating trust, 166–167
  design of experiments, 131–132
  eliminating barriers to change,
    114–115
  helped by Total Leadership program,
    3–4, 6
  stakeholder performance expecta-
    tions, 85–86
  stakeholder performance gaps, 86–87


"Tanaka, Kerry," 53, 187, 189
  description of future, 29–31
  description of hero, 37–38
  finding common ground, 111–112
  focus on learning, 195

reflection on four-way view, 180–181
synergy of intentional change,
  179–180

"Washington, André," 187, 189
  description of hero, 38
  experimentation by, 147, 149–151
  focus on learning, 195
  helped by Total Leadership program,
    4–6
  leadership lessons, 185–186
  optimism, 193
  preparation for stakeholder dialogues,
    104
  reflection on experiments, 177
  relationship among domains, 68–69

*Note:* Page numbers followed by (*fig.*) indicate illustrations.

*Achieving Success Through Social Capital* (Baker), 163
action learning, 171–172
action metrics, 141
  examples of, 144–145
  observation of, 142
  reflection on, 175
adjustment to unexpected
  gaining commitment by, 169–170
  in implementing experiments, 151–155
  metrics useful for, 156
"angry" relationship pattern, 90
Apple Computer, Inc., 34
Appreciating and Caring experiments, 125
  action metrics for, 144–145
  in community domain, 134–136
  "architecture of time," 130
  art of "interruptability," 130
assessments
  of satisfaction, 67–70
  of stakeholder expectations, 89–90
AT&T, 126
attention, allocation of
  difficulty of paying attention, 129–130
  Focusing and Concentrating experiments, 125–126, 145
  four-way attention chart, 56–60
  psychological interference and, 68
authenticity

achieving through writing, 62
  clarifying important issues, 29–51, 69–70
  coaches and, 203
  as core value, 10
  four-way view and, 53–70
  importance of, 34
  leadership and, 188–189
  practice of, 2, 9, 10
  in Total Leadership program, 212

Badaracco, Joseph, 33
Baker, Wayne, 163
balance
  difficulty of achieving, 54
  search for, 9
  "work/life balance," 14, 15, 17
  zero-sum solutions, 88
barriers to change
  confronting, in experiments, 169
  eliminating, 114–115
baseline, revisiting, 24, 184
Bono, 157
boundaries, 84–85
  effective management of, 86
  experiments in managing, 128–129, 173–174
brainstorming, 131, 214
broken trust, 115

career objectives, achievement of, 5–6
change
  awareness of need for, 206–207
  behavioral, 129
  fears and anxieties about, 202
  inevitable risks of, 136
  intentional, promotion of (*see* intentional change)
  in leadership vision, 42
  meaningful, imagining, 31
  social change, ethics and, 19
  torrid pace of, 20
clarification of important issues
  authenticity and, 29–51, 69–70
  core values, 45–49
  examples of story, 34
  exercises, 31, 32, 41, 46–48, 51
  in experimentation, 121–122, 129
  four-way attention chart and, 63–64, 64 (*fig.*)
  leadership vision, 39–45
  personal history and, 32–38
  reflection, 50
clients, coaches and, 203, 204–205
coaches, 19, 22–23, 135
  authenticity and, 203
  dos and don'ts for, 209–210
  exercise, 194
  professional, 202
  responsibilities of, 204–205
  wholeness and, 203–204
coaching
  directive, 203
  nondirective, 203
coaching networks, 50, 201–210
  benefits of coaching, 202–204
  challenges of intentional change, 206–209
  creation of, 22–23, 204–205
  dos and don'ts of, 209–210
  effective feedback from, 202–203, 205–206
commitment, passionate, 167, 172, 188
commitment building, 98, 137, 149–170
  by adjusting as needed, 169–170

exercises, 152, 161–162, 165–166, 168
  impact of actions and, 167–169
  inducing reciprocity, 162–164
  in intentional change, 208
  leadership leap, 156–159
  by network building, 164–165
  political point of view, 159–162
  stakeholder dialogues and, 149–151, 158
  "trust market" and, 166–167
common ground, finding through stakeholder dialogues, 110, 111–112
communication
  with coaching network, 205
  face-to-face, 92, 101
  forms of (exercise), 93
  with key stakeholders, 11
  media for, 91–94
  relationships and, 155–156
  tools for, 11, 20, 174–175
community domain, 56
  contribution to, 150
  experiments in, 134–136
  impact of everyday actions, 167–169
  key stakeholders in (*see* key stakeholders)
  results metrics, 143
  shift in awareness and, 169–170
continual adjustment, 153
continuous learning, 187, 193, 195
core values, 45–49
  alignment with vision, 182, 183 (*fig.*)
  exercise in, 46–48
  identifying and using, 70
  review of, 180–184, 183 (*fig.*)
courage, as core value, 49
creativity. *See* innovation

decision to act, 207
"defining moments," articulation of, 33–34
Delegating and Developing experiments, 126–127, 145
delegation of tasks, experiments in, 125–127

DeLuca, Joel, 159, 160–161
digital technology, 91
    effects on productivity, 92
    technological slavery and, 20
direct benefits of experiments, 123–124,
    134
direction, choosing, 98
direct support, 163
disconnection, feelings of, 6–7
*Discovering the Leader in You* (Lee
    and King), 46–48
dissatisfaction, effects of, 3–4
domains
    boundaries between, 84–85, 86,
        128–129, 173–174
    changes in, 57, 60
    defining, in four-way view, 55–56
    defining goals for, 138–140
    effects of performance on, 111
    flexibility of, 85, 120
    four circles graphic, 60–67
    four-way attention chart, 56–60
    incompatibility of, 62–63
    integration of, 190–191
    as life system, 84–88, 150–151
    merging, 128–129
    multiple-domain perspective, 88–89
    psychological interference between,
        68, 130
    relationships among, 57, 60, 68–70
    satisfaction and, 68–70
    segmenting, 129
    single- and multiple-domain experi-
        ments, 123–124
domain satisfaction, 67–70
    exercises, 67, 70
    relationship among domains and,
        68–70
"dreaded stakeholder," 53–55, 105, 110
Drucker, Peter, 19

Eisenhower, Dwight D., 159
"elixir of negotiations," 108–109
Emerson, Ralph Waldo, 16

emotional intelligence theories, 16
"enlightened self-interest," 159–160
ethics, social change and, 19
everyday actions
    alignment with values, 182, 183 ( *fig.* )
    impact of, 167–169
"expansive" relationship pattern, 91
experiments. *See* Total Leadership ex-
    periments
Exploring and Venturing experiments,
    127
    action metrics for, 145
    in community domain, 134–136
"explosive" relationship pattern, 90

face-to-face (F2F) communication, 92,
    101
failure, value of, 133, 161, 176–177
family
    as core value, 49
    influence of, 36, 37, 38
family (home) domain, 56
    building trust in, 113
    experiments in, 132–136
    incompatibility with work domain,
        63–64, 64 ( *fig.* )
    intentional change in, 65
    key stakeholders in ( *see* key
        stakeholders)
    performance expectations in, 178
    results metrics, 143
fears and anxieties
    about experimentation, 146–147
    about process of change, 202
    about stakeholder dialogues, 98,
        103–106, 116–117
    addressing, 214
    fear of writing, 41–42
    psychological pressure cooker, 90–91
feedback
    from coaching network, 202–203,
        205–206
    as subjective metric, 141
    "360-degree feedback," 99

*Finnegans Wake* (Joyce), 199
flexibility of domains, 85, 126, 145
Focusing and Concentrating experiments,
  125–126, 145
four circles, 60–67
  alignment of values and vision, 182,
    183 ( *fig.*)
  exercise, 61–62
  learning from, 63–67, 64 ( *fig.*), 66 ( *fig.*)
  overlap in, 62–63, 66 ( *fig.*), 66–67
  review, 183–184
four-way attention chart, 56–60
  examples of use, 58–60, 63–67, 64
    ( *fig.*), 66 ( *fig.*), 182, 183 ( *fig.*)
  exercise, 57–58, 180
  review of, 180, 181
  as subjective judgment, 56–57
four-way happiness rating
  as assessment of satisfaction, 67–70
  exercise, 67
four-way view, 10, 53–70
  defining domains in, 55–56
  domain satisfaction, 67–70
  exercises, 57–58, 61–62, 67, 70
  four circles, 60–67
  four-way attention chart, 56–60, 180, 181
  revisiting, 180–184, 183 ( *fig.*)
four-way wins, 2, 88–90
  "enlightened self-interest" and,
    159–160
  exercises, 131
  identification of (exercise), 131
  planning experiments for, 123, 127–133
  pursuit of, 14–15
  synergy of intentional change, 179–180
  Total Leadership experiments, 11–12
  valued goals and, 12–13
  in work domain, 211–215
Freud, Sigmund, 18
Friedman, Stewart D., 68, 130, 159
future transformation, vision of, 44–45

game plans for experiments, 135
Gardner, Howard, 33

Gardner, John, 18
gender equity, 19
general metrics, 143
globalization, pace of change and, 20
goals
  change in order to produce harmony,
    64–65
  defining for each domain, 138–140
  establishing (exercise), 24, 184
  expressing, 205
  path-goal leadership model, 16
  problem solving in accomplishment of,
    208
  recording (exercise), 139, 140 ( *fig.*)
  reflection on, 173–177
  sharing with key stakeholders, 132
  of stakeholder dialogues, 97
  stating explicitly, 24–25
  valued goals, four-way wins and, 12–13
Greenhaus, Jeffrey H., 68, 130, 159
Gregory, Joe, 214
guilt, anxieties and, 146

harmony in life
  improving, 2
  study of, 1
health and well-being
  improvement in, 8
  improving, 2
  pace of change and, 20
  psychological pressure cooker, 90–91
  regular exercise, 125
heroes
  descriptions of, 37–38, 161
  story of (exercise), 32
Heschel, Abraham Joshua, 130
honesty, as core value, 49
human capital movement, 18
human potential movement, 16–17
hybrid experiments, 124, 134–136

ignorance, fear of experimentation and,
  146

"I have a dream" speech (King), 33, 39, 40

incompatibility of domains, 62–63

individual, importance of, 20–21. *See also* self domain

individual achievement
  of four-way wins, 15
  Total Leadership and, 5–6

individual contributors, 13

industrial models, destructiveness of, 17–18

innovation, 11–12
  coaches' help with, 204
  experiments in (*see* Total Leadership experiments)
  gaining commitment for (*see* commitment building)
  practice of, 2, 9, 11–12
  reflection and growth, 192–194
  in Total Leadership program, 213–215

inspiration, as core value, 49

integrity, 10–11, 73–95
  coaches and, 203–204
  defined, 73
  identifying key stakeholders, 75–77
  leadership and, 189–192
  practice of, 2, 9, 10–11
  respecting whole person, 73–95
  stakeholder dialogues, 97–117
  in Total Leadership program, 213

intentional change
  awareness of need for, 206–207
  barriers to, 114–115, 169
  challenges of, 206–209
  created by leadership, 4
  decision to act, 207
  as goal of Total Leadership program, 64–65
  large-scale, small wins and, 138
  meaningful, imagining, 31
  promotion of, 18–19
  results of, 9 (*fig.*), 187–194
  sense of urgency for, 207, 214
  "small wins" approach, 149–151

of stakeholder expectations, 97
sustainable, 198–199
synergy of, 179–180

interests
  difference between underlying and surface, 106–107
  finding common ground, 110
  reciprocal display of, 114
  serving others, 161–162
  uncovering shared, 108–109

internal conflict, learning to resolve, 3–4

"interruptability," 130

isolation, feelings of, 6–7


Jobs, Steve, 34
Joyce, James, 199


*kaizen*, 193
Kennedy, John F., 164

key stakeholders
  benefits of experiments for, 157–158
  dialogues with (*see* stakeholder dialogues)
  "dreaded stakeholder," 53–55, 105, 110
  exercises, 76, 78–80, 86, 93
  expectations of (*see* performance expectations; stakeholder expectation analyses)
  gaining support from, 75, 112–115
  help with experiments, 128
  identification of, 11, 75–77
  media for connecting with, 91–94
  relationships with, 74, 90–91
  selection of, 100
  sharing goals with, 132
  stakeholder performance gaps, 86–88
  what they expect of you, 77–81
  what you expect of them, 81–84

King, Martin Luther, Jr., 33, 39, 40
King, Sara, 46–48

law of reciprocity, 163
leaders
    effective, nurturing of connections
        and, 126
    focus on others' needs, 156–158
    learning and, 141
    nature of, 13–14
    passionate commitment of, 167
    religious leaders as exemplars, 62
leadership
    at all levels, 13–14
    authenticity and, 188–189
    choosing to lead, 21, 24
    creation of change, 4
    fundamental challenge of, 98
    integrity and, 189–192
    nature and importance of, 16–17
    path-goal leadership model, 16
    as performing art, 9 ( *fig.* ), 187–194
    redefining, 12–15
    study of, 1
    trait theory of, 16
*The Leadership Engine* (Tichy), 37
leadership leap, 156–159
leadership lessons
    examples of, 185, 186, 191–192, 196
    reviewing, 185–187
leadership stories, 196–197
leadership vision, 39–45
    articulation of, 10
    communicating with passion, 45
    compelling story of achievable future,
        39–40
    core values aligned with, 182, 183 ( *fig.* )
    described in writing, 40–42
    discussing in stakeholder dialogues,
        101–102
    example of, 42–45
    exercise, 41
    as opportunity to dream, 40
    review of, 180–184, 183 ( *fig.* )
*Leading Minds* (Gardner), 33
lean manufacturing, 8
learning
    action learning, 171–172

in becoming leader, 141
from four circles, 63–67, 64 ( *fig.* ), 66
    ( *fig.* )
life-long, 187, 195
in Total Leadership program,
    212
Lee, Robert, 46–48
life system
    domains as, 84–88, 150–151
    as garden, 198–199
Limited Brands, 156

manipulation, 160
Marx, Karl, 16
meaningfulness, importance of, 18
media for communication, 91–94
merged domains, 128–129
metrics
    action metrics: examples, 144–145
    devising, 141–143
    in making adjustments, 156
    objective, 141
    observation of, 142
    reflection on, 173–177
    results metrics: examples, 143–144
    specific, 143
    qualitative, 142
    quantitative, 142
middle managers, 13
"moral block," 160
multiple-domain perspective, 88–89

networks
    coaching networks (*see* coaching net-
        works)
    cultivating, 163
    online networks, 23
    open approach to building, 164–165
Nooyi, Indra, 157

online network, 23
optimism, 193

organizational loyalty, disappearance of, 20

organizational psychology, 17

organization structures, flattened, 20

organization theory, 19

path-goal model of leadership, 16

patterns

in relationships of domains, 84

in stakeholder relationships, 90–91

PepsiCo, 157

perceptions, of broken trust, 115

performance

effects on other domains, 111

experiments in, 128

improvement in, 2, 8, 181

increasing capacity for, 199

keeping log of, 124

stakeholder performance gaps, 86–88

performance expectations, 12

assessment of (see stakeholder expectation analyses)

for coaching networks, 205

example of, 85–86

key stakeholders and, 74, 78, 79 (fig.)

leadership lessons, 185–186

new, negotiating, 101

revisiting, 177–180

stakeholder dialogues and, 104–111

stated as surface needs, 106–107

unification of, 85–86

verifying and changing, 97

what stakeholders expect of you, 77–81

what you expect of stakeholders, 81–84

performance log, 124

permeability of domains, 84–85

perseverance, value of, 37–38

personal growth, 18

personal history

in clarification of issues, 32–38

exercise, 32

pilot programs, 214–215

Planning and Organizing experiments, 124, 144

Plato, 16

political point of view, 159–162

Political Savvy (DeLuca), 159–160

"positions," performance expectations stated as, 106–107

"positive spillover," 88

preparation for stakeholder dialogues, 100–102, 116

example of, 104

exercise, 102–103

spirit of inquiry, 105, 109

pressure, reducing, 114

"pressure/guilt" relationship pattern, 90–91

problem solving, in intentional change, 208

psychological interference between domains, 68, 130

psychological pressure cooker, 90–91

public policy ethics and, 19

quality-control programs, 8

quantifiable results of Total Leadership program, 7–8

"rational block," 160

reciprocity, inducing, 162–164

reflection, 50, 171–199

on clarifying motivations, 50

exercises, 51, 116–117, 174, 178, 180, 184, 185, 194, 197

four-way view, 180–184, 183 (fig.)

further development and, 194–196

goals and metrics, 173–177

leadership lessons, 185–187

leadership stories, 196–197

results of change, 9 (fig.), 187–194

return to baseline, 184

stakeholder expectations, 177–180

sustainable change and, 198–199

reinforcement of intentional change, 209

Rejuvenating and Restoring experiments, 125
  action metrics for, 144
  in community domain, 134–136
relationship among domains
  changes in, 57, 60
  domain satisfaction and, 68–70
relationships
  Appreciating and Caring experiments, 125, 134–136, 144–145
  communication and, 155–156
  considering, in stakeholder dialogues, 102–103
  experiments in, 132–133
  improving, 8
  key stakeholders, 11, 73–74
  leadership leap and, 156–159
  media for connecting, 91–94
  patterns of, 90–91
  revealed in stakeholder dialogues, 99
  strengthening through storytelling, 196–197
  success in, 74
  understanding one's place in, 204
religious leaders as exemplars, 62
resistance
  minimizing, 186
  overcoming, 151
  persisting in face of, 146–147
respect, as core value, 49
results metrics, 141. *See also* metrics
  examples of, 143–144
  observation of, 142
  reflection on, 175
Revealing and Engaging experiments, 126, 145
Rogers, Carl, 18
role reversal exercise, 110
role theory, 17

Sabbath observation, as time allocation, 130
satisfaction
  assessments of, 67–70

effects of dissatisfaction, 3–4
  increase in levels of, 8, 181
Schlesinger, Len, 156
scorecard, 138–145
  action metrics: examples, 144–145
  defining goals for each domain, 138–140
  devising metrics, 141–143
  exercises, 139, 140 ( *fig.*), 146, 152, 174
  results metrics: examples, 143–144
  in small-wins approach, 137
segmented domains, 129
self domain, 56
  improving satisfaction with, 8
  performance expectations in, 178
  Rejuvenating and Restoring experiments, 125, 134–136, 144
  removing guilt, 159
  results metrics, 144
  transformation in, 188
self-interest
  eliminating, 157
  political point of view and, 159–160
self-knowledge, pursuit of, 18, 21
self-revelation, 38
  reciprocal display, 114
  Revealing and Engaging experiments, 126, 145
  in stakeholder dialogues, 99
sense of true purpose, establishment of, 5–6
sense of urgency for change, 207
Shell, Richard, 108
Six Sigma, 8
"small-wins" approach, 19
  commitment building and, 151–156
  effectiveness of, 151, 154
  to experimentation, 136–138
  leading change and, 149–151
  pilot programs, 214–215
"smart experiments," 11–12
social capital
  benefits of, 164–165, 170
  law of reciprocity and, 163–164

marketplace for trust and, 166–167
social change, 19
social impact of actions, 167–169
social intelligence theories, 16
spirit of inquiry, 105, 109
stakeholder dialogues, 94, 97–117. *See
also* key stakeholders
building and restoring trust, 112–115
coaches' help with, 203–204
commitment building and, 149–151,
158
with "dreaded stakeholder," 53–55
exercises, 102–103, 108–109, 110,
116–117
finding common ground, 110, 111–112
gains from, 98–100
goals of, 97
handling anxieties, 98, 103–106,
116–117
locations for, 101
meeting expectations through, 106–111
preparation for, 100–105, 109, 116
surprises in, 104–105
stakeholder expectation analyses,
89–90, 169
coaches' help with, 203–204
four-way wins and, 179–180
stakeholder expectations chart, 78, 79
(*fig.*), 81, 82 (*fig.*), 86, 91, 177,
178–179
stakeholder performance gaps, 86–88
stakeholder relationships. *See*
relationships
storytelling
benefits of, 196–197
building connections with, 191
compelling story of achievable future,
39–40
importance of, 32–33, 36–37
personal history, 32–38
in writing (*see* writing)
"structural holes," 164–165
subjective metrics, 141
success
of others, contributing to, 163–164

in relationships, 74
sharing, 162
small wins and, 137
support
from coaching network, 201, 205
direct and indirect, 163
gaining from key stakeholders, 75,
112–115
storytelling and, 196–197
surface needs, performance expectations
stated as, 106–107
sustainable change, 198–199
systems analysis, 17

"testing the waters," 107–109
Thoreau, Henry David, 16
"360-degree feedback," 99
Tichy, Noel, 37
time
allocation of, 69, 124
"architecture of time," 130
intelligent use of, 6, 8
"time bind," 68
Time-shifting and Re-placing experiments, 126, 145
top executives, 13
Total Leadership, 1–25
authenticity and (*see* authenticity)
future of, 19–20
practicing, 9 (*fig.*), 9–12
quantifiable measures of, 7–8
redefining leadership, 12–15
results of, 3–9
sources of, 15–19
Total Leadership experiments, 121–147
adjustments made in implementing,
151–155
benefits for key stakeholders,
157–158
confronting barriers to change, 169
courage to experiment, 121–123
example of, 134–136
exercises, 131, 133, 135, 146
generating ideas for, 127–133

Total Leadership experiments (*continued*)
　impact of, 213
　indirect benefits of, 123, 134
　multiple domain, 123
　single domain, 123
　small wins, 136–138
　"smart experiments," 11–12
　specific goals and metrics for (*see*
　　scorecard)
　types of, 123–127
　will to experiment, 146–147
Total Leadership program
　being real, 212
　four-way wins with, 211–215
　help provided by, 3–6
　innovation, 213–215
　intentional change as goal of, 64–65
　quantifiable results of, 7–8
　steps in, 98–99
　wholeness, 213
Tracking and Reflecting experiments,
　124, 144
trait theory of leadership, 16
trials, framing experiments as, 137–138
trust
　building or restoring, 112–115, 155, 160
　as core value, 49
"trust market," 166–167
24/7 availability, 20, 92, 130

U2, 157
Ultimate Frisbee club experiment,
　134–136

verification of expectations, 97
vision. *See* leadership vision

Wharton School, 8
wholeness. *See* integrity

*Work and Family—Allies or Enemies?*
　(Friedman and Greenhaus), 68, 159
work domain, 55–56
　alignment of values and actions, 182,
　　183 (*fig.*)
　building trust in, 113
　creation of new sectors in, 150
　experiments in, 128, 174–175, 176
　four-way wins in, 211–215
　incompatibility with family domain,
　　63–64, 64 (*fig.*)
　intentional change in, 64–65
　key stakeholders in (*see* key
　　stakeholders)
　results metrics, 143
workforce, demands of, 20
"work/life balance"
　advocates of, 15
　as field of research, 17
　as zero-sum game, 14
work persona, redefining, 35–36
Wright, Frank Lloyd, 73
writing
　in achieving authenticity, 62
　diary of thoughts, 142
　distillation of leadership lessons,
　　185
　fear of, 41–42
　idea lists, 50
　"I have a dream" speech (King), 33,
　　39, 40
　leadership stories, 197
　leadership vision described in,
　　40–42
　notes on stakeholder dialogues,
　　116–117
　performance log, 124
　preparing for stakeholder dialogues,
　　103
　storytelling, 32–34
www.totalleadership.org, 23, 24, 32, 135,
　　139, 173, 201, 210

STEW FRIEDMAN joined the Wharton School faculty in 1984. He became the Management Department's first Practice Professor in recognition of his work on the application of theory and research to the real challenges facing organizations. He is the founding director of both the Wharton Leadership Program and the Wharton Work/Life Integration Project. In 2001, Stew concluded a two-year assignment (while on leave from Wharton) at Ford Motor Company, where he was the senior executive for leadership development. In partnership with the CEO, he launched a corporate-wide portfolio of initiatives to transform Ford's culture, in which over twenty-five hundred managers per year participated. Following these efforts, a research group (ICEDR) described Ford as a "global benchmark" in leadership development.

Stew's writings on leadership development and succession, work/life integration, and the dynamics of change include the widely cited *Harvard Business Review* articles "Work and Life: The End of the Zero-Sum Game" (coauthored with Perry Christensen and Jessica DeGroot) and "Be a Better Leader, Have a Richer Life," and, in the *Academy of Management Executive*, "The Happy Workaholic: A Role Model for Employees" (with Sharon Lobel). His books include *Integrating Work and Life: The Wharton Resource Guide*, in which he co-edited (with Jessica DeGroot and Perry Christensen) the first collection of learning tools for building leadership skills that integrate work with the rest of life. *Work and Family—Allies or Enemies?*

(coauthored with Jeff Greenhaus) was recognized by the *Wall Street Journal* as one of the field's best. His national bestseller, *Total Leadership: Be a Better Leader, Have a Richer Life*, has sold over sixty thousand copies, is now available in six languages, and is the basis for a massive open online course (MOOC) that reaches tens of thousands worldwide (on coursera.org). Stew's latest book, *Baby Bust: New Choices for Men and Women in Work and Family*, is a landmark twenty-year longitudinal study that revealed surprising differences between Gen Xers and Millennials.

Stew has advised many organizations, including the U.S. Departments of Labor and State, the U.N., and two White House administrations. He gives high-energy keynote speeches, conducts interactive workshops, and is an award-winning teacher. The *New York Times* cited the "rock star adoration" he inspires in his students. He was chosen by *Working Mother* as one of America's twenty-five most influential men in having made things better for working parents and by Thinkers50 as one of the "world's top 50 business thinkers." The Families and Work Institute honored him with a Work Life Legacy Award in 2013. Follow him on Twitter @StewFriedman. Tune in to his show, *Work and Life*, on SiriusXM 111, "Business Radio Powered by the Wharton School," Tuesdays at 7:00 p.m. (EST).

Stew played music and drove a taxi in New York during college and for a year thereafter, then worked for five years as a mental health professional in Vermont and New York before earning his PhD (1984) in organizational psychology from the University of Michigan.

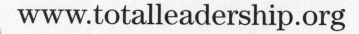

# www.totalleadership.org

*Improving performance in all aspects of life—work, home, community, and the private self (mind, body, spirit)—by creating mutual value among them*

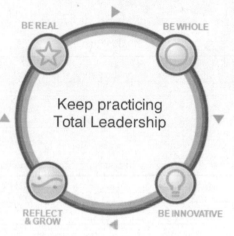

- Access tools you can use
- Learn about inspiring experiments others have done
- View alumni and other videos
- Keep up-to-date: blogs, research, media coverage, news, events, and more

**Compose and share your four circles at myfourcircles.com**

- **What my four circles say:** Size the circles to show the relative importance of your domains then click and drag them to show their alignment

- **What I'm working on:** Identify experiments to improve alignment and score a four-way win

- **Ask your community:** Get help from others on the design and implementation of your experiments

## Stew Friedman | Founder, Total Leadership

Stew brings inspiring passion and practical ideas for action.

With his worldwide experience as a successful leader of change in organizations for three decades—he's an accomplished executive, award-winning educator, widely-cited researcher, sought-after consultant, high-impact coach, and dynamic speaker—he knows how to help people in organizations produce sustainable results.

Invite Stew to your group or organization to improve performance at work, at home, in the community, and for the private self (mind, body, and spirit). He will show you how to score four-way wins with Total Leadership in a way that makes sense for you and the most important people in your life.

info@totalleadership.org

610.664.2387 (USA)

www.totalleadership.org